Phoenix Rising

- Overcoming Obstacles -

Erin Michelle

Phoenix Rising

Overcoming Obstacles

2022 © Erin Michelle

All rights reserved. No reproduction, distribution, or transmission of this publication in whole or in part is permitted without the written consent of the author, except for quotations in book reviews and interviews.

ISBN

Paperback: 978-1-7782985-0-9

Author Contact

erinmd@telus.net

This book is dedicated to everyone who's endured hardships and risen above them. My hope is that you find you are not alone and are supported in your own journey within these pages. May you always arise stronger than before…

I wouldn't be where I am today without the love, guidance, and encouragement of my dearest friends, Renee and Megan. Their unconditional support has made me who I am today.

E.M.

Table of Contents

Part One: How it All Began

Chapter One: Fighting to be Heard

Chapter Two: Longing to Belong
- The Black Sheep
- The Mute
- The People Pleaser
- Fight, Flight, or Freeze

Chapter Three: Toxic Relationships
- The Baba
- The Drunk Narcissists
- The MIL
- Myself

Chapter Four: Body Image Issues
- The Struggle of a Lifetime

　　　　The Ups and Downs
　　　　Why Me?
　　Chapter Five: Internalizing it All

Part Two: But Wait, There's More

Chapter Six: The Stroke
　　　　But I'm Only 30!
　　　　Aha Moments
　　　　What Do You Mean I'm Pregnant?!
　　　　Rush to Recover

Chapter Seven: Chronic Fatigue Syndrome
　　　　How it All Began
　　　　What is Going On?
　　　　Okay, I'm Not Fine
　　　　Queen Bee
　　　　I'm Losing Everything
　　　　My Life is Over

Chapter Eight: The Darkness
- The Spiral
- Medication Upgrade
- What Quality of Life?
- Dark Night- Part One
- Dark Night- Part two
- Unit 91

Chapter Nine: Borderline Personality Disorder
- Oooooohhh, That Makes Sense
- Haven't I Been Through Enough
- Great, So I Have No Feelings?

Chapter Ten: The Chameleon
- Really?! Me Too!
- What Opinion?

Part Three: Stepping Into My Own

Chapter Eleven: Breaking Toxic Patterns

    External Validation

    Addictions

    Coaching, Mentoring, and Counseling

Chapter Twelve: Finding Myself

    What?! I Have a Choice?

    Finding My Inner Child

    Balloon Family

    Listening to My Heart and Getting Out of My Head

    Believing in Myself

    The Water, The Trees, and Me

Chapter Thirteen: Who I Am Now

    The Sum of All Parts

    Anything is Possible

    The Witch, The Lion, and The Phoenix

Part One
How it All Began

Chapter One: Fighting to Be Heard

Do you ever feel like you're in the middle of talking and nobody's listening? Well, you're not alone in that. I've spent a lifetime trying to be heard.

A little background may help to understand. First, I'm the oldest of five siblings. This inherently came with the role of babysitter when my parents needed the assistance. The only trouble with the arrangement was that my younger siblings didn't necessarily feel like following me as the authority figure. I never understood why, as I was a diligent rule follower and took my role seriously, ensuring I channeled my parents' expectations to a tee. Perhaps I was seen as a buzz kill because anything I said was ignored. In reality, the next siblings in line ran the ship, and I didn't seem to even exist. I tied my worth to how well I played my role. I didn't know until much later in life that I was worthy simply by existing, by being me, not because of what I did. The dynamic left me feeling like an utter failure as I wasn't fulfilling my assigned duty as babysitter. I was letting my parents down, but more on the people pleasing me, later.

This was a trend that followed me throughout life. Whether it was with peers, when teaching, or as a parent, my words went without being heard. I was

Phoenix Rising

talked over, talked back to, challenged, or simply ignored. Eventually, I stopped trying as it just seemed like I was wasting my time. I learned to just shut my mouth and say nothing. I played small and shut off my voice. There was so much I had within me to express and share, and I denied myself that right. Ringing any bells? Stay tuned, I'll share with you how I eventually found my voice in the upcoming chapters.

Chapter Two: Longing to Belong

Kids can be mean, man. That's my experience, anyhow. Being bullied is a special kind of hell. I'm certain we have all experienced it to some degree, and my heart goes out to all of you who've been subjected to it. It shapes part of our identities, whether we know it or not, and takes a lot of work to get over. In my case, I never knew what I was going to get. The basis of being picked on was so random, and very often, contrary. There was no way to win.

I felt picked on for simply being me. Whether it was my clothes, glasses, braces, hair, it didn't matter. I also did very well in school and was separated from my classmates to attend an enriched program. I felt this also made me stand out from others when all I wanted to do was fit in. I remember feeling on edge more often than not, anxious, waiting for the other shoe to drop. I denied myself the feeling of joy and didn't allow myself to shine. I didn't embrace my uniqueness or share my authentic self with others as I felt vulnerable and that I wouldn't be accepted. I also had a difficult time identifying who I, Erin, truly was until much later, as I instead tried to fit in to the group. Some of factors I feel may have contributed are mentioned below.

The Black Sheep

I never identified with my peers, no matter what age I was at. Perhaps being the oldest in the family played a role, as I didn't relate to my siblings, either. From as young as I can remember, I felt like I was standing on the other side of the glass from others, not knowing how to interact or reach them. I was an old soul, preferring to sit quietly and observe my parents and their friends conversing, over playing with toys or play make believe. Truth be told, I never knew how to play. I passed my time with my nose in a book instead. I would see other kids playing with ease and I'd wonder how they did it. I'd try but I just couldn't figure it out. This left me.

The Mute

Once school began, the process of making friends was awkward. I couldn't relate to the lives others lived, although I tried. They seemed so foreign, so exciting, especially those who grew up in town. I grew up on an acreage in the middle of the jack pines, miles out of town, and nowhere close to others. I had my family for company and that was about it. As I learned how the town kids got together all the time, establishing friendships early on, I already felt left out. How could I talk to these people when I had no idea how to relate? So, I stayed quiet and just listened to their stories. I was shy, and familiar with that. It seemed safe and I could stay in my comfort zone.

This was seemingly a great technique as we progressed throughout our school days, as how could I be bullied if I didn't provide any ammunition? Well, by staying quiet was reason in and of itself.

Again, I chose to stay small and deny my voice. I realize now, how much I played the victim... I trapped myself in the vicious cycle of believing the hurtful words of others and internalizing them. I didn't believe in myself or allow my soul to sing. I was as much a source of my own repression as the people who picked on me. I was my own bully. This was something I repressed for nearly 40 years. I have found my voice in recent years, and it feels amazing to speak my truth and share my opinions and ideas with the world. The difference now, is that I feel safe to do so and have come to realize that it doesn't matter what others think of me as long as I am true to myself. Wouldn't that be amazing to do as a child? To be true to yourself and be uniquely you right from the start?

I am seeing this more and more in the younger generations and applaud it. Not only are these children being themselves and speaking their truths, they are being encouraged to do so. What a gift it is to feel safe to be yourself! This is something I encourage in my own children as I don't want them feeling the way I did growing up. I want them to shine and embrace their uniqueness, sharing their gifts and magic with the world, not suppressing themselves for the sake of others.

The People Pleaser

My go to attempt to fit in was people pleasing. I was, and still am, a natural at that. I'm an obliger, rule follower, and want to make people happy. I'm a yes girl to a tee. This, I'm sure comes as no shock, that I did so at my own detriment. I wouldn't dare speak my own mind, as it seemed that going with the flow was far more advantageous. If I went along quietly, even when it went against my own nature, I found that the bullying was less frequent. If I gave people what they wanted, what could go wrong, right? Well, as it turns out, people only want so much of that. Then it became an endless well of bullying as the other kids found it humorous that I tried so hard to befriend them. And, oh, did I try.

I tried to fit in in all sorts of ways, but I was awkward to say the least. I tried to be like them by liking their music, which was pop, and I grew up on Kenny and Dolly. I did follow Michael Jackson and Debbie Gibson, but that was the extent of my coolness.

Your appearance is an opportunity to express yourself, your uniqueness. In my growing up years, I wasn't in touch with my authenticity, so I didn't express myself well at all. I also didn't have a say in what clothes I got. But, those were the times.

I wanted the cool clothes, you know, the brand names like Club Monaco and Guess, yet in reality, I much preferred clothes that had no branding on them, and I could never afford them anyhow. My mother would go to into the city for three days every August to buy all our school clothes, so I wore what she bought until I was in high school. Hand me downs were like Christmas day, as there was the chance that I wouldn't be dressed only by Zeller's. Talk about feeling awkward. My wardrobe was a very easy target for the bullying.

Then there was the hair. Going through school in the 80's was an experience, let me tell you. My mom cut my hair until I hit junior high, and I had two prominent hair styles, the girl mullet and the all-one-length style. Now, my hair is fine, but I have a ton of it. It's whack-a-do curly/crinkly, and back in those days, hair straighteners weren't invented yet, so my hair was all over the place. The trending style was the big, backcombed, Aquanet glued, mane. Well, with the weight and length of my hair, all I achieved was a giant rat's nest. Awesome, right? Well, that's what happens when you try to figure things out on your own. There were no YouTube tutorials to refer to back then, it was a trial and error thing. So, teasing resulted. And I really couldn't blame them because even I could see how bad it looked.

Glasses and braces were the icing on the cake. I still remember to this day what my first pair of glasses looked like. They were the size of basketball hoops, clear acrylic with baby blue top halves and baby pink bottom halves, beauties! That, they were not, but there was only so much in the clearance section to choose from. They were a statement, that's for sure. I remember returning to school the next day to stares and snickering. What can you do, not wear them and be blind as a bat?

Although much of this was simply the way it was, I also played a part in shutting my authentic self down. I talked negatively about myself, a pattern that has only been broken in recent years. I was only adding to the hurt I felt by being my own worst critic. I was always putting myself down and was ashamed of myself. What a terrible energy to put out into the world. Oh, how I would've done things differently if I'd known then what I know now, but that is all part of my journey. Does anyone relate to allowing negative or hurtful words into your consciousness, and then begin to believe them to the point that you are telling yourself the same things? What a toxic cycle it is. The worst thing we can do is deny our uniqueness, our authentic self, and once we allow it to shine, we can fully live the life we are meant to live. Otherwise, we are simply existing.

Fight, Flight, or Freeze

Going back to the basics, and I'm talking caveman days here, humans have an involuntary physiological response to a perceived stress. Most people are familiar with the fight or flight responses, but there's a third, freeze. Who knew? They are fairly straight forward concepts, in my mind, but let me give a brief review of each just for fun.

Fight is how we physically defended ourselves from danger. When the caveman met with a wild animal, they ran into the face of danger. Fight is what kept them alive, and often fed. It determined the alpha, and it settled arguments. Now think of today's society and the attraction to MMA. People like to beat on each other, and even more people enjoy the show. This, however, is very much not me, but you might identify with this method of coping.

Flight is another way we defend ourselves. Rather than running into danger head on, we run the other way. Staying out of the fray kept people safe, and therefore, alive. Nothing wrong with that, is there? Again, not me. But, is it you?

Freezing is the third way people react to stress. This is often recognized as the deer in the head lights response. When a person is faced with a threat, instead of fighting their way out of it or running away from it, they simply freeze. They are paralyzed in the moment.

Now this is me. I am the person that freezes up. My face turns red, I get hot and sweaty, my ears ring, and my vision and hearing go in and out. I'd just stay wherever I was at, and simply take whatever was dished out. I would never have survived as a caveman, that's for sure. I'd have been a delicious snack for the first carnivore I encountered. As brutal as being bullied was, at least I wasn't devoured by my peers, not physically, anyhow.

I coped by just taking it. I didn't fight, I didn't run, I just endured whatever the torture was on any given day. Sometimes it was being laughed at, sometimes being screamed at, and other times, it was both. I was an easy target, I soon learned. But I couldn't do anything about it as my reaction was instinctual, not a choice I made. I wish I could have responded differently, but that just wasn't me. With each incident, I was acutely aware of being the center of attention. The helplessness that I felt as I saw the delight on people's faces as they picked me apart, and heard the cruelty in their laughs, was like nothing else. I had nowhere to go and nobody to turn to. Does this hit home with any of you? If so, know you couldn't have done any different. We all do the best that we can, and that's all we can expect of ourselves. Congratulations for getting though it, I know it couldn't have been easy.

I have learned however, that although I physically froze, I could have helped myself by not internalizing the hurt. I allowed it to get into my core and believed the lies my mind told me about myself. Now, I talk to myself lovingly, and show myself compassion and grace when drama creeps into my life. I have also learned to set personal boundaries and

Phoenix Rising

boundaries with others to honor my energy, my heart, and my soul. I have become my own cheerleader and best friend. As long as I am happy with myself, that is ultimately all that matters. It took me a long time to learn this, and takes practice, but my goodness is it a life changer.

Chapter Three: Toxic Relationships

Toxic relationships are those that are detrimental to a person, whether it be physically, mentally, or emotionally. Bullies are toxic people, but kind and loving people can be toxic, too. In essence, if you are being minimized or made to question your worth in any way, you ought to question whether you're interacting in a toxic relationship. Another thing to note is that someone toxic to me, may not be toxic to you. It's about each individual relationship. It took me many years to recognize this fact.

It also took a lot of work to understand my role in these relationships. Because of my insecurities, of not being heard or seen, and my inability to speak up for myself, I contributed to the below issues because I came from a place of feeling powerless and worthless. It is a large part of why these relationships were so significant.

The Baba

So, this girl is Ukrainian, and for those of you who are of similar descent, you know who Baba is. For those of you unfamiliar with the title, she is the grandmother, the family matriarch, the revered one. I had a Baba that I adored as a child, and I'd do essentially anything to please her. She played an influential role in my early development, as well as later in life.

Phoenix Rising

From as far back as I can remember, I can recall her teachings and contributions to my upbringing, and I took to heart anything she had to say. This was a double-edged sword, however. I vividly remember the praise that went to my siblings and cousins, and even more vividly remember how hard Baba was on me in contrast.

Perhaps she figured I knew she loved me, but apparently, I missed the memo. Baba showed her love by correcting me every step of the way, especially when it came to my weight. I was chastised if I did something wrong, yet the other kids didn't seem to experience the same. You know how they say the oldest gets it the hardest because the parents are learning on them? Maybe this explains the double standard. All I know is that I had the pleasure of listening to my baba praise everyone else, including kids outside of the family, but all I heard about myself was how I could be better.

This was particularly hurtful as I sought to please her so much. I was an honors student, followed the rules, and wouldn't dare do anything wrong. But I was flawed. I was overweight, and man, did I hear about it. Every time I would visit, I would hear, "hello, I see you've gotten bigger, better start watching what you're eating". Ouch. It was very much a sore point when I got to hear my siblings be greeted with, "hi sweetheart, you're looking so good. I hear you just got student of the week!" Like really?! If it was once or twice, I'd understand, but… Every. Single. Time.

When I had my first boyfriend, my Baba blatantly voiced her disapproval of him at an Easter gathering to my aunts, who were in our immediate vicinity. She didn't even try to be subtle about it. I was mortified, embarrassed, and stunned. I mean we were very much able to hear every word. Most people would pull others to the side and quietly speak their minds. Nope. Baba didn't give a damn who heard her. Yet, when it came to anyone else's relationships, they could do no wrong, and only praise was given.

And yet, I still tried to please, tried to seek her approval. I spent thirty years trying to do so, to no avail. Even when I lost weight, it went without acknowledgement. No matter what I did or how hard I tried, I could never satisfy her.

The one time I heard through word of mouth that Baba was impressed with me, was when I went back to my nursing practicum a mere two weeks after having a full hemiplegic stroke (more on that later). I can honestly say it shocked me, and I wasn't sure how to process it. Why couldn't I please her when everyone else seemed to do so with ease?

Her tough love hit the very core of my insecurities. I felt uncomfortable in my own skin, so her words cut like a knife. She was my idol, and I felt I continually let her down. Because of my lack of self-love and self-worth, I allowed the opinions of others dictate how I felt, when I should have built up my own self confidence rather than seek it from others.

The Drunk Narcissists

Speaking of my first boyfriend, I must admit that it wasn't the best decision I ever made. My Baba was right about him. I should have trusted my first instincts and turned him down. But I was naïve, a nineteen-year-old farm girl living in the big city. I didn't have any experience dating. I went to school with the same people my entire life, graduating in a class of fourteen, the smallest in the school's history. I knew nothing of the dating world, and I was taking my friends' word on how that all went. What could go wrong? My friends encouraged me to accept a date, so I did. At first, he seemed like a decent guy, but what did I know?

Now, a bit about narcissism is pertinent here. It includes a sense of self-importance and lack of empathy for others, never believing they're wrong and having things their way. They are manipulative, possessive, and controlling. My boyfriend had a heartbreaking story of hardships and being done wrong by. And I fell for it hook, line, and sinker. Within the first month, he proposed, and I was so surprised and happy that someone wanted me that I said yes. I didn't realize that this proposal was merely a way to control me and claim ownership over me. Looking back, there were early warning signs, but I didn't see them until later. It wasn't until I met his family that I got a more rounded account of the man's true self.

As it turned out, he had a talent for twisting every situation to make himself the victim, when in most cases, he brought his issues upon himself by making poor decisions. I got to witness this for myself as our relationship progressed. It was always somebody else's fault, and he was always the innocent. To add to the drama, the man couldn't hold down a job, and had a nasty drinking problem. He would become so drunk, that he couldn't function. Yet this was somehow my fault, go figure. He could go out any time, with anyone, but the one time I went out with the girls which I told him about beforehand, I came back to him sitting in his apartment lobby with a clock in his hands, grilling me about being out, and for being out without him. When I worked as a server in a restaurant, he'd come sit at the bar, buying drinks on my dime, watching me work. Controlling much?

    I was in university at the time, relying on my minimal student loan and a weekend waitressing job, living in my grandparents' basement. He was relying on me to support him. See anything wrong with this picture? It took me a while to figure it out, but I eventually got there. I was hung up on the notion that I'd made my bed and it was my obligation now, to lay in it. That there was no going back. That I wasn't allowed to admit I'd misjudged the man, and that I couldn't get out of it. And I was ashamed that I made the mistake of being with him intimately.

    I was raised that you didn't have sex until you were married, and I'd gone against that. I felt so much guilt and shame in that decision, that I was causing my own suffering. I was putting expectations above what was best for myself. I felt stuck, that I didn't have a choice but to carry on. My ego was telling me that I'd made the choice and there was no going back, when my heart had been screaming to be free from him for the longest time. I believed that this was a mess that I had created and, therefore, had to clean up and make right. But this was conflicting with what my heart was telling me… that I deserved peace, real love, and happiness.

As we nearly reached the year mark, I'd had friends and family pulling away, had several people voice their concern for me, and I saw the writing on the wall myself. But I wasn't sure how to correct the situation. He'd manipulated me by threatening to kill himself when I tried to cut ties previously. Talk about guilt tripping. After a few rounds of this, I eventually realized that I wasn't ever going to help him if he wanted to truly end his life, and I needed to do what was best for me. My ego and self-esteem took a real beating over the course of that relationship. For a girl who was bullied throughout school, I fell into the same thing in my first relationship. I had no voice, was belittled and berated, and was worrying those who loved me. Ending the relationship with him was a huge step in realizing my self-worth and that I didn't have to sacrifice myself for the sake of someone that was no good for me. Talk about toxic. If only I'd known how to speak up for myself at that time.

During the course of writing this book, I was in another relationship, one that mirrored the above relationship. Again, I found myself with a controlling, manipulative, jealous individual, who slowly but surely isolated me from my world. The worst was the anger issues he had. Now, I'd had twenty some years of getting stronger and standing up for myself and wouldn't tolerate the mental and emotional abuse of being screamed and sworn at. We were together a year, got married, then three and a half months in, I promptly left as I recognized the toxic relationship for what it was. I didn't see it until I saw it, but when I did, there was no hesitating, I got the hell out.

As I reflected on repeating the pattern of being with a narcissist, I saw that these two weren't the only ones. I'd, in fact, been in relationships, both romantically and with friends that were also controlling, manipulating, and emotionally and mentally abusive. My boundaries with others were non-existent, and my own boundaries were also weak. I put myself into situations where I thought I was loved, and was seeking to be loved, because I hadn't yet discovered that within myself. It was easy for me to believe the lies they told as I wanted so much to believe I was beautiful, worthy, and lovable.

Once I filled these needs within myself, I've attracted the right individuals into my life. Those that support and love me like I deserve to be loved, and who encourage me to be the best I can be rather than the narcissists that kept me small. My boundaries protect me from those that seek an easy victim, and I am no longer desperate for love as I love myself.

The MIL

The next relationship I had, was a set up through a friend. I hadn't dated a soul after the narcissist, but that was due to not having a clue how. So, in my last year of university a classmate asked if I'd be interested in meeting a friend of her husband's as she felt we'd hit it off. Well, he was a great guy, and this time, trusting my friend worked in my favor. We were married for sixteen years before we divorced. We are still great friends to this day.

This was not so much the case with his mother. At first, we got along alright, me being a teacher as she and her husband were. It's always good to have something in common. Establishing a relationship with in-laws has that honeymoon stage that a romantic relationship has. You know what I mean, the phase where everyone is polite and feeling each other out. Inevitably, this period cannot last forever, and personalities begin to clash.

The turning point for us was when children entered the picture. I don't know about you, but as a parent I took it very personally when my authority as Mom was disregarded. It was a direct blow to my ability to parent, it undermined my authority, and it confused my children. Again, it triggered the insecurities I carried from my childhood… that I wasn't good enough, that I wasn't being heard, and that my opinions and even my presence didn't matter.

Examples ranged from who determined the food on my children's plates, me knowing which foods they'd eat or not eat but her still serving said foods anyhow, ultimately having it go to waste. I'd say no to a treat immediately before dinner, and she'd sneak them the cookie anyhow. The worst example of disregarding my parenting was when one of the boys was given a time out on the time out bench. She was made aware of the fact that he was in a time out, and she decided to sit down and take selfies with him. I mean, who does that? I'd had it and I was sick of having my parenting toes stepped on.

I was frustrated and angry, and when I expressed my desire for her

to respect my decisions as the mother, they were blatantly ignored. To further add insult to injury, I asked my ex-husband to step in to support me, as we were a parenting unit, and restate the concern to his mom. He didn't see the extremity of the issue in the same way I did, and that it was up to me to make things work out. He was staying out of it. I felt betrayed, that my supposed partner didn't have my back, and despite all my efforts, his mother continued to act in the same way. Without support or a change in her behavior, I got to the point where she was no longer welcome in my house. It was my safe place, my sanctuary, and I had had enough of feeling invisible in my own home and to my family.

I never kept the kids or my husband from visiting with his parents, but it was done without me present. This was not their issue, but my own, and I strongly believe in the rights of children spending time with family that love them. The relationships they had with their grandma are healthy ones. My relationship with her was the toxic one.

Phoenix Rising

This was the first time I really set boundaries. I needed peace and all I felt when we visited, was stress and anxiety. Perhaps to others, the above issues don't seem like a big deal, but to me, they continued to open old wounds, wounds that had not yet been healed. To me they were a big deal, and I was hurt, angry, and felt defeated. I needed time to heal and feel that I was being heard, was being respected, and that I mattered. It made all the difference in the world. My anxiety eased tremendously, and I learned what it was like to have a voice.

Myself

We all have an inner child, that part of ourselves that came into this world pure and perfectly untainted. Unfortunately, this part of us doesn't stay untouched for long. The moment we start to experience the world, we hear things, see things, feel things, and begin to internalize what we are learning. From a very early age, this inner child of mine was lost within the deepest parts of me. She hid from the scathing remarks she heard around her, the criticism she faced, the feeling of not being enough, and everything else that felt threatening. She coped by hiding, hiding deep within. When she retreated, so did the childlike behaviors, the make believe, and the play. That part of me was gone and I was a grown up at a very young age.

Now, this part of me can't be blamed for retreating, not one bit. Because for as insecure as she was, I wasn't doing my part to protect her. I was toxic to myself. Instead of nurturing her, standing up for her, comforting her when she was afraid or hurt, I did nothing. I didn't know how to help her, as I felt overwhelmed and hadn't even recognized she had gone. I was barely getting through the days as it was, so how was I to help this inner part of me that I wasn't even aware of? Oh, if I'd known then what I know now, things would've been different. But it wasn't, and my inner child was hidden for nearly forty years before I became aware of her presence and her needs.

I was as toxic to myself as others were toxic to me. I believed the bullies, that I had no self-worth. I believed the body shaming, the teasing, the fact that others mattered more than I did. I'd worsen my situation by eating away my emotions, by distracting myself from that voice inside, longing to be heard. Instead of combating the negativity thrown my way, I was soaking it all in. I didn't believe in myself or that I had any worth to others. Worst of all, I didn't believe I had any worth to myself.

When you don't feel you are worthy, a person tends to give up on themselves, perpetuating the situation. It was a very deep hole I found myself in as I kept absorbing all the negativity, and when you're used to the negativity, you refuse to accept anything positive that comes your way because you're so deeply conditioned that you aren't worthy of it. You don't see that you are worthy, simply for being you. You treat yourself with disdain and dislike, and you make all sorts of choices that reflect how you feel about yourself. You hold yourself back because you can't possibly be good enough to have what you really want. What a sad position to be working from. Yet so many of us find ourselves there.

I was nearly forty years old before I began to see I had worth, worth from within, not just for what I could do. I discovered I had this long-lost inner child who needed me. And I started listening. I came to understand how she protected me by taking the pain deep into the depths with her so that I could function. Now, it was my turn to return the favor and work systematically through the emotions one by one and make her feel safe. This was certainly not an overnight process, but slowly and surely, I began to see myself through different eyes, through loving eyes, and they were turned towards that wounded inner child. To this day, I continue this work, asking myself what that inner child needs, and going from there. In large part, she is responsible for this book.

Chapter Four: Body Image Issues

I'm certain that I'm not alone in the fact that I've struggled with body image issues. Whether it be weight, looks, acne, being too tall, being too short, curly hair, straight hair, or any of the countless issues there are out there, everyone has had a moment where they've wished they were different. How can we help it when the idea of body perfection is constantly thrown in our faces from airbrushed magazines, to television, to social media, to children's toys, and so on? The expectation to be perfect is out there, barraging us constantly. As I mentioned earlier, I didn't even need those external sources, as I got it from within my own family. It is shocking how little it takes to become conscious of one's image, especially if you don't fit the mold. And of course, the more you're exposed to the messaging, the more you internalize it all. Entire books and courses are dedicated to this topic, so I'll just get to how it played into my story.

The Struggle of a Lifetime

I'm sure if I asked you right now, you could name something you would like to change about yourself, right? But as a youngster, I couldn't see other girls' insecurities, so I didn't know that we were silently fighting the same battle, I only knew my own struggles. As far back as I can remember, I've had body issues. I can't remember a time that I didn't have negative beliefs about my looks. The moment self-awareness came into the picture, I felt flawed. The flaws weren't targeting one area, but many areas at the same time. As a young girl this was devastating, and I felt isolated in my imperfections. I believed everyone else was so pretty, so perfect, yet here I was, the flawed misfit. I don't have a single school picture I smiled in, as I just never felt good enough about myself to do so.

My hair was the first thing I felt subconscious about. I had a ton of it, and it was unruly, so my mom cut it short in the front to tame it some. Yes, it happened, I had the female mullet for years, and no, it didn't tame my hair one bit. Remember, too, this was long before hair straighteners or high-heating curling irons were available. I relied solely on what a brush could do. Not much, let me tell you, and I've got all the school pictures to remind me. I think my best look was in grade 6, when back-combing was the thing. Unfortunately, I had nobody to teach me how to actually pull off this look properly, and I just ended up with a rat's nest on top of my head. This particular year's photo was accentuated with braces and glasses, just to add insult to injury, but I'll get to those next. Thankfully, the perm was in style, and my mom was able to perm my hair herself, which I was so grateful for. It saved me from further years of hair agony.

So, several things happened to me at the same time. I hit puberty, needed glasses, and had to wear braces. What a combo that was! Not only were the fashion trends for clothes and hair not on my side, neither were glasses. Mine were these huge acrylic frames with baby blue on the top and baby pink on the bottom. Braces, well, enough said there. But puberty, what a joy that was. I gained more weight, had new body odor, would sweat like crazy, and developed acne and unwanted facial and body hair. I remember my mom pulling out a long, black hair from my chin, calling it a witch hair. That one statement has never left my mind, and I've diligently plucked my chin multiple times a day ever since. Now, I realize the medical need for glasses and braces, but in terms of the hit to my self esteem, it all worked together in this perfect storm to knock it down. Nothing was as poignant as my weight, though.

My weight was, and still is, the biggest issue I've had with my body. As early as four years old, I felt I stood out. I was in both gymnastics and dance, and I was very aware of the fact that I was larger than my peers. I had to wear bigger sizes, my tummy stuck out, my legs touched, and I was always hidden in the back. In dance, especially, I was acutely aware of my size as only the smaller girls got solos or got to do lifts. As I got older, I refused to take dance, as my body issues were at the forefront, and it took away the joy I'd once had in participating. When other sports replaced dance, my weight again interfered with my enjoyment of the sport. I'd wear three pairs of tight leggings under my baseball uniform to control the iggling. I'd be more concerned about my tummy and how it rolled over my XL pants, than I was about the game. I was athletic, but my inner thoughts controlled my ability to engage fully. Looking back, what a shame it was to mute my joy of athletics for the sake of looks.

This was true for my daily attire as well. I'd be completely preoccupied with how things tucked or bulged, and what others thought of me, that I was continuously fidgeting with my clothes. The size, being XL, felt awful to have to wear, and I couldn't stand the look of my body. I was broad and curvy when all I wanted to be, was thin. Not super thin, just not pudgy.

I was forever hearing remarks comparing me to my tinier siblings, cousins, or friends. Weight was made something of great importance in my family, whether it was realized or not. I know how much of an impact it made on me, that's for sure. I know I wasn't the only one, however. I watched my dad deal with his own body issues, and I happened to have his body type. I watched him as he'd diet and make sure to exercise. And I followed suit. I did what I saw. If it worked for him it should work for me, right?

This was about the same time my long-time doctor weighed me at my regular spring checkup and said, "I see we've been enjoying our Easter treats." Really?! Did he actually just say that to me? I shut down, my ears rang, and frankly, I don't remember the rest of that day. I was mortified. Even the doctor thought I was fat. I'd just had my worst fears validated, by a doctor no less. I don't know if he ever realized the impact he had on me that day, but I sure do. It was one thing to hear comments made around me, but this was flat out telling me to my face that I was heavy. It was a huge blow, and it defeated me. So, at twelve years old, I saw the new doctor in town to get on a diet plan.

Think about that for a moment. I was twelve! And in hindsight, not particularly overweight, just a bigger framed kid. But I'd already been conditioned to hate my body. I felt like a skinny girl trapped in a fat girl's body. This feeling held true most of my adult life as well. Can anyone else relate to not identifying with their bodies in that, or any other way?

Even now, my weight is a struggle for me. I tied my worth with my body for so long, that I'm still working on detangling the two. I've had a tummy tuck, breast surgery, Botox, and fillers to feel more like myself. They were effective, for sure, but they don't last forever. As I wrote parts of this book, I was the heaviest I've been to date, and it was tough. Even though I know better now, I still found myself falling into old trains of thought. But I am a lot better than I was.

I couldn't believe, let alone accept the compliments I received over the years. They seemed so at odds with the other messaging I received, especially from myself. I couldn't see the beauty others saw in me and I questioned their sincerity.

Now, as I've been working on self-love and compassion for myself, the weight has been coming off. I look at myself with loving eyes, accepting and adoring the skin I'm in. I am not perfect, but I look at myself in the mirror and see the way I shine, the way I glow, the love I have for myself instead of the flaws. My weight was a form of protection, like armor against the abuse I'd faced. Now I thank it for its role and have told the weight that I'm safe now. Its listening and I am healthier for it. I shower myself with love, kindness, and praise.

The Ups and Downs

For so long, I was uncomfortable having my picture taken. I avoided the camera as much as possible. This was due to my distorted body image. I'd envision that I looked one way, then was taken aback when the camera captured me differently than the way I saw myself in my head. It's the strangest thing when I could see myself in the mirror and be good with what I saw, then moments later, feel all my flaws come to the forefront when the camera flashed.

There are three times in my life where I felt like that skinny girl inside. The first was when I'd just graduated university, and worked out every day, accompanied by clean eating. I was getting married, and wanted to look my best, so I did everything within my power to do so. I got myself down to 150 lbs. The second time was when I was in my mid-thirties and worked with a trainer to again get my weight down. The regimen was very similar to the first time I succeeded. This time, I got to 140 lbs. Not bad after three kids and fourteen years since being that low. The third time was at forty, returning to 140 lbs after being sick and unable to do anything for three years.

As thrilled as I was during these periods, and as camera friendly as I was, these times didn't last. They couldn't possibly as the methods I used to achieve my success wasn't healthy or realistic. Exercising doesn't always equate to being healthy. This is also true for "healthy eating". From the first time I went to the doctor for a diet plan, I was going about things the wrong way. I was dieting, a temporary plan to lose weight, and I was starving myself. No wonder the moment I ate something substantial, I gained weight. As I mentioned earlier, my weight shifted as I wrote this book, and I'll be honest, it bothered me at the beginning. Mostly because I successfully sustained 140 lbs for three years before Covid came in and my patterns changed. The frustration came from having what I wanted most and letting it slip away. This turned to my favorite, although previously unrecognized, pattern of stress eating. That, my friends, is how you create a mountain out of a mole hill. I just dug myself a deeper hole by eating away the loathing I felt for myself for allowing myself to gain weight. So, the cycle continued. The biggest realization I had was my unhealthy relationship with food, and until I learned to see food differently, I wasn't going to break the pattern.

Now, I eat when my body tells me I'm hungry. I allow myself to have whatever my body calls for. I find that now, that I'm not hungry like I used to be. A big part of this change is that I am not carrying the stress I did before. I'm also listening to my heart and

Phoenix Rising

doing the things that make me happy. To overcome my toxic body image issues, I booked a boudoir shoot, even though I was well over 200 pounds at the time. I trusted the photographer and was part of her Facebook group which focused on the beauty within, regardless of size. The amazing women in the group radiated beauty in all shapes and sizes, and the body positivity was off the charts. With all the inner work I was doing to love myself and become empowered, when the day my photo shoot came, I was so ready for it! I was radiating beauty, and it wasn't because my body was perfect, it was because I came to love it no matter what size or shape it was. I had the best time that day, embracing my glorious self. I even jumped at the opportunity to take nude photos! The day I got to view the images, I cried. I loved Every. Single. One. I bought the entire package. I often look at those images, adoring the empowered woman I see in them. I am so grateful that I followed my heart and did the photo shoot. I saw the beauty within, and the outer beauty, too. The secret, I've learned, is that self-love is the key to true beauty.

Why Me?

As I grew up, I always came back to the question of why me? Why did I have to deal with all these issues when others didn't? It felt incredibly unfair to be dealt this hand. Why couldn't I have been blessed with the genetics of other family members? Why did I get all the difficult issues? I felt cursed and like I had to deal with everything alone. Life felt unfair, especially during my school years as all my insecurities led to bullying. There must be a reason, right? For the longest time I didn't have the answer to that, but eventually I had some crucial realizations. Stay tuned, I'll disclose all my secrets shortly.

I did come to understand I was not alone in my insecurities, tons of other people I knew had them too, but nobody talked about it. It was such a relief to know I wasn't alone, and over the years, I learned techniques for dealing with my insecurities. And thankfully, braces only lasted a few years, contact lenses became my eyewear of choice, I learned how to dress myself, and how to style my hair.

I feel confident and beautiful. I feel worthy of compliments. I feel comfortable in my own skin. And I have never felt better.

Chapter Five: Internalizing it All

Children are so impressionable, and I was no different. When adults, especially, spoke, I took their words to heart. I did so with peers as well, but the grown-ups I revered and respected made the most impact. This was even so when I wasn't the person of interest, but merely overheard comments about weight, looks, etc. uttered about someone else. I made the mental note that I better not be like so-and-so. I literally feared doing, saying, or being anything like the people I heard talk of.

Ironically enough, by fearing these things, I brought energy to them and manifested these issues into my own life. I became my own worst nightmare, and internalized all the shame, guilt, and unworthiness. This isn't to say anyone went out to make me feel this way, I did it to myself. I had many loving messages throughout my life. I was told I was beautiful, especially my eyes, but I was at odds with these compliments as I had taken the negative to heart so much. What you give your energy to is what you take in, and for me, it was the harmful messages I allowed take over my mind, body, and soul.

My mind was always preoccupied with all the ways I wasn't good enough. I would dwell on that negative self-worth day after day, stuffing these feelings further and further down. I didn't know appropriate coping skills for these things. It certainly wasn't taught in school, and the belief of the time was to tough it out and it'll get better. Anyone else been told to tough it out or suck it up? Helpful advice, isn't it?

My body collected stress like a magnet. I carried it everywhere in my body and was always sore and achy. My body also deals with stress by holding onto weight, which furthered the problem. Stress eating didn't help matters either. I put so much stress on my body that I accumulated a series of health issues, which I will explain in detail in Part Two. It wasn't until I was in my 30's that I learned how my thoughts affected my body and how to manage it.

My soul, the precious entity that it is, took a beating along with the rest of me. Little by little, I lost my spark, my appreciation for the magical being that I am. Pieces of my soul broke away and were buried where they would be protected from the barrage of pain I was amassing. I felt like a mere shadow of the person I was meant to be. My heart literally hurt, and pieces of it, too, hid deep within, protecting itself the only way it knew how.

The little girl within, the one I mentioned earlier, was now buried so deep, I had forgotten all about her. I only felt emptiness and loneliness, and was stuck in that for years, not knowing how to get out. I was coping with everything by using my own devices, which got me nowhere.

I've learned the value of self-love. This I cannot stress enough. No amount of work you do for yourself will help you until you can see yourself through

Phoenix Rising

loving eyes. Show yourself the kindness and compassion that you'd show to your child or best friend and start speaking to yourself that way. The toxic thoughts we are conditioned with need to be unconditioned. This doesn't happen overnight, but it is possible. Replacing the negative thoughts with positive ones teaches your body and mind that you are worthy of the compliments and you will wake up one day loving yourself, having removed the false stories you've told yourself for so long. It really does change your view of yourself.

Part Two
But Wait, There's More

    The Universe has a funny way of making you pay attention to your issues if you haven't been. I'm a firm believer that our bodies turn emotional stressors into physical ailments and illnesses. There is no hiding from, or denying, the things that have affected us emotionally because if we do, we then also end up dealing with physical issues. This is no fault of our own, we don't mean to sabotage and make things worse for ourselves, we just generally don't realize the connection.

    A simple example of this is when a person is doing too much for others and is forgetting their own self-care. They tend to have shoulder tension and pain, a physical manifestation of literally carrying too much on their shoulders. It takes some practice to catch onto these connections, but once you do, it's a real game changer. Then you can ask yourself what your physical pain is trying to get you to pay attention to emotionally.

    I wasn't the fastest learner, and it took a ton of small ailments and several major physical illnesses for me to comprehend the amazing connection between our emotional and physical wellness.

    The first major issue I had was a life-threatening stroke, which you'd think would be a big enough warning, but no. Eight years later, my body shut down again, this time with Myelo-Encephalitis, also known as Chronic Fatigue Syndrome. The toll this illness took on every aspect of my life then led to a deep, dark depression, all of which I'll go into detail within the following chapters.

Chapter Six: The Stroke

After a brief teaching career and giving birth to our first son in 2005, I was mere months away from being able to work in my dream career as a Registered Nurse, one that I was finally accomplishing in my thirties, and I couldn't be happier. As my ex-husband and I lived in mid-central Alberta at the time, I'd returned to my parents' place to be closer to school. What a blessing that turned out to be.

The morning of June 28, 2008, was a morning none of us will ever forget. My alarm went off this Saturday morning, and I was excited to get ready for the fourth shift of my final nursing practicum. As I was getting out of bed, I found myself on the floor. Odd, I thought, but I must have gotten myself tangled in my bedding and as a result, fell. Ok, not a problem, I was in the basement, using an air mattress, so I wasn't far from the floor anyhow. Now to get myself back on my feet and get going for the day. Hmmmmm… why is this not working? My legs didn't seem to want to cooperate, so I tried to get onto my hands and knees, thinking I could then get up from there. But no go. What the heck? I've got to get going, already, as I'm not one to be late, especially to work. I felt fine, so why was my body not cooperating? Aaaaaand now I've got to pee, fantastic. Nothing like adding urgency to the situation. At this point, I realized I was going to need some help, so I tried to call my dad, who's usually up early. It took nearly a dozen attempts before he came to investigate the noises from the basement. Meanwhile, I had also been trying to drag myself to the bathroom, so I could pee, with little success.

Now what you have to understand is that I felt perfectly fine. My brain was not informing me that anything was wrong. In fact, I felt ridiculous having to call for help because for some reason, I couldn't get off the floor. I was athletic, eating healthily, and in perfect health. It made no sense that I would find myself in this predicament.

Well, as soon as my dad found me, the look on his face said it all. Something was wrong, very, very wrong. He immediately instructed Mom to call 911. This is bad, we never use 911, we just drive to the hospital, which is only blocks away. Why was 911 necessary? Then I heard Dad also direct Mom to call ahead and ensure that the doctor, who'd normally come in for 7 am rounds on the weekend, would be there upon our arrival because I'd had a stroke. Stroke? What was he talking about? That's ridiculous, I didn't have a stroke, yet my very intelligent parents were reacting like I did. Mom was getting me to stick out my tongue, say sentences, lift my arms, and the like, so I humored her and played along with these basic stroke assessments.

Remember how I said my brain was telling me I was fine? Yeah, this is where my mind was playing tricks on me. I thought I was passing all these silly tasks with flying colors, and in the meantime getting annoyed that nobody was paying attention to my need to pee. Turns out I was wrong, very wrong.

The ambulance attendants had now arrived, and their faces mimicked those of my parents. The concern was apparent. It really started to sink in when I arrived at the hospital, and the nurse and doctor were just as concerned, if not more so. They were so worried for me that the biggest debate was how to get me to the trauma center in Edmonton. Would it be by STARS, our air ambulance, or by ground?

Now, the irony was that I should have been one of the nurses working the shift instead of being the patient brought in on the stretcher. As I witnessed them urgently start IV lines and insert a catheter for me, I was fascinated with how much I was learning about emergency nursing. I still felt oddly fine and wasn't comprehending all the fuss, but what did I know? For those of you following along with my priority to pee, thankfully the catheter relieved that.

Ultimately, ground ambulance was deemed the faster route, so, with my dad at my side, I was strapped into the ambulance and was raced to the University of Alberta emergency department. During travel is where I began to lose track of events as I kept falling asleep. I don't know if I lost consciousness or not, I just know that I kept waking up and going under again. I remember a few odd turns or bumps in the road, but it seemed like no time before I found myself being assessed at hospital number two.

For accuracy, despite feeling normal, I actually suffered a hemiplegic stroke. What this means is that I was completely paralyzed on my right side, my face was droopy, my arm and leg didn't work, and nobody could understand a word I said. Far cry from being fine, huh? No wonder everyone was freaking out. It was discovered through a series of tests that a clot lodged itself in my cerebellum, the motor control center of my brain. I was given a mega dose of a clot-busting medication, and I improved by the hour. I was still going in and out throughout all this, and don't have much recollection of the order or timing of things.

But I'm Only 30!

Given my partial memory of all the details, I won't try to put them all in order. The sum of it was I spent the Canada Day long weekend in emergency, awaiting a bed in neurology and the reopening of diagnostic departments on the following Tuesday. The question I, and everyone else had, was how I could have a stroke in the first place? I was only thirty years old, and a very healthy thirty, at that. I didn't have any risk factors for a stroke, so how did this happen?

I spent a week in the hospital, completing an array of tests, which was absolutely fascinating to me. Yes, I'm a huge medical nerd, so witnessing my own testing and treatment had me geeking out. I had a neurological team assessing me as I was apparently a medical mystery and they were not going to release me until they had some answers. Okay, great, I didn't mind a bit. I too would like to know what happened and why. I was learning so much about myself, and by the end of it, I can say with great confidence, that I had the most thorough work up imaginable. The team didn't miss a thing.

It was remarkable to the medical team that, a) I had such a massive stroke at only thirty years old, and b) I recovered so dramatically. As it turned out, I had a small hole in between the top chambers of my heart, called an atrial septal deviation (ASD), which allowed a clot from somewhere else in my body to travel to my brain, where it got stuck. This resulted in a butterfly-shaped dead spot in my brain. Neat, huh?

So, it was concluded that the stroke was a medical phenomenon, that it should never have happened, nor should it ever happen again. What a relief! The hole in my heart was subsequently closed to ensure there were no repeat events, by the way. I wasn't taking any chances. After a week, I was discharged, saying that I should go live my life, and not worry about reoccurrences.

Aha Moments

I believe things happen in our lives to teach us, and the stroke was a big one. I remember the first day in emergency, saying to my husband at the time, that I wasn't ready to go yet, that I had more to do and experience. Our son was only three and a half, and I wanted to see him grow up. I wanted more children, and I wanted more time to do all the things I dreamed of doing.

I also came to recognize how loved I was, as I had hordes of relatives come in to visit me, all with great concern on their faces. Even my home-bound grandparents, the Baba that I spoke of earlier, went to great lengths to come to the hospital to see me. The gravity of the state I had been in was becoming apparent as people pieced the series of events together for me.

I almost died. My dad was bargaining with God to keep me alive, my family was making critical life-saving decisions on my behalf as I was incapable of doing so myself, and I was unaware of it all. I wish I could have saved everyone the heartache and worry they went through, but I was unaware of all of this until after the fact.

It was the oddest realization to be told how near to death I was, and yet feel like I was maybe a little bit tired. That's all I experienced, was being drowsy. I had no pain, no sense of being as disabled as I was. My brain didn't compute that my limbs weren't moving, or that I couldn't be understood by a single person. I don't know a better way to describe it, but to say it was surreal. I experienced the bizarre truth that I couldn't trust my own brain like I once did, as it had let me down. I've questioned my reality ever since. I regularly check if my perception of events is indeed accurate as I didn't trust myself anymore.

What was my body trying to tell me? Well, I needed to get out of my head and stop trying to overthink everything. I needed better balance in my life, not just the constant go, go, go pace at which I was doing things. I was doing so much for other people, I wasn't allowing myself the care I needed. The right side of our body is where our masculine energy resides, the action, the doing part of us. The left side is the feminine domain, one of receiving, rest, healing. I was living an unbalanced life. I wasn't paying attention to the feminine energy that was calling me to take care of myself.

What Do You Mean I'm Pregnant?!

After all that I had just been through, oddly I hadn't been scared. I felt that I would be alright, and so I didn't worry. That is until the day, about a month after returning home from the hospital, when I discovered I was pregnant. I wanted to be happy, but I had just had a stroke and I was terrified the doctors would tell me it wasn't safe for me to carry a baby at this time.

I was never as relieved as the day my doctor said that I was safe to be pregnant. It was about a week after taking the home test then getting the bloodwork conformation, when he gave us the good news. Until that point, I'd been holding my breath, scared of what he'd say, not to mention trying to wrap my own head around it. The doctor even teased my then husband, asking him if he'd jumped me in the hospital bed as we'd gotten pregnant so quickly after my release from the hospital. We all had a good laugh about that. It was a joyous day, indeed, when he gave me the all clear and congratulated us. That being said, being pregnant did present some additional challenges to my recovery.

    I was still coming to terms with post-stroke life, the symptoms and effects that could linger, sometimes for years, and my brain had essentially just undergone an electrical reset. Now, for those of you who have been pregnant or heard the stories relating to pregnancy, you're likely familiar with the quirks that come with it. Compound pregnancy with post-stroke issues, and you've got yourself some good fun. Try distinguishing memory loss and emotional ups and downs being because of the stroke or because of pregnancy. To this day, there are so many overlapping symptoms I'll never know what came from what. It's not that I really needed to know, but it sure made doctor appointments, follow ups, and overall symptom tracking cloudy at the time.

Rush to Recover

    I was also extremely eager to return to my practicum, as there was a deadline by which it had to be completed. I'm also not one to sit still and doing so was making me antsy. Thankfully, after a mere three weeks, I returned to my practicum, pregnant and all, and I completed it within the timeline to graduate.

Even after the stroke, I went full steam ahead, into my practicum, with baby number two, and then returned home and worked in a hospital setting. Within two years, our family moved to just outside of Edmonton, where I worked full time, had two children, and a third on the way. Even three children didn't slow me down. I transitioned from a hospital nurse to working in home care, and I was a full-time wife and mother. I was loving my life and thriving. I cherished my nursing career, and truly enjoyed every day I went to work. I took on whatever was asked of me, and never said no.

In hindsight, there was still so much going on with my body that I should have given myself more time. I wasn't listening to the message that I needed to slow down and take care of me, I was still pushing things down, not listening to my body, and pushing through to get things done. I hadn't learned the lesson that led to the stroke in the first place… that I was doing too much and pushing too hard. I continued taking care of everything like nothing ever happened, so the Universe sent me another message.

Chapter Seven: Chronic Fatigue Syndrome

I feel it is important to give a little insight on what Myelo-Encephalitis or Chronic Fatigue Syndrome, ME/CFS for short, is. When I mention that I have Chronic Fatigue Syndrome, ninety nine percent of the time, the response is, "yeah I get really tired, too." Now, this is meant in a sympathetic way, but the reality is that ME/CFS is far from simply being really tired.

This is an illness that debilitates the person who has it, often leaving them bed-ridden and unable to do anything for themselves. The body simply shuts down and doesn't want to work anymore. There is not a lot known about how ME/CFS works within the body, and every diagnosis is unique in the symptoms presented. There are a few defining tests that validate the diagnosis of the disease, and very few doctors who are even knowledgeable in the area. As with many obscure diseases, ME/CFS is more a diagnosis of ruling out all other possibilities first. Then, if you are one of the fortunate ones, you are assessed by someone who is aware of the syndrome and can determine if your symptoms indeed match the criteria they have. Sadly, there isn't more information or support out there, as ME/CFS still has so little known about it.

There is a consensus however, that the syndrome has two triggers. Either it follows some sort of trauma, like a car accident, for example, or it is as a result of a viral infection. Now, these incidents do not cause the illness, but they are believed to trigger the dormant illness within someone who is susceptible to having it.

How it All Began

I'd been living my life for seven years after my stroke and feeling I had finally hit my stride. The boys were at a point where they were a little more independent and in school, and I was performing my dream job, loving every minute of it. I enjoyed my colleagues, my clients, and every element of what my work entailed. I had been working out and taking care of myself, and this was one of the times I loved the skin I was in. I was living my dream.

I even participated in a body building competition, training vigorously and diligently at the gym six days a week and succeeded in releasing fifty pounds. I was motivated, felt amazing, and was so proud of my accomplishments. I pushed my body hard, but it felt so good to do so.

In the spring of 2015, there was a particularly nasty flu virus that went around. Most everyone in the office contracted some form of it, and although I was only mildly affected by it, that was all it took. I was working the May long weekend and found myself feeling run down. I just didn't have my normal stamina, so I took some time off from my workouts to rest and get over the virus. This was an annoyance, albeit a minor one, as I enjoyed my time on the treadmill or with the weights. Little did I know that I would never be able to tolerate those activities again. So much for a minor inconvenience.

    It took a few weeks for me to feel up to working out again, as the flu virus was one that lingered. When I finally went back to the treadmill, I was shocked to only have the capacity to endure three minutes at, for me, was a crawling pace. Now, I realize that when you return to exercising after a bit of time off, you'll have a bit of regression, but this was ridiculous. I was panting, and my legs felt like lead. At first, I attributed this to still fighting off the flu, but when I made several other attempts over the course of a few more weeks with no better results, I realized something was wrong. I'd even begun to find walking throughout the course of a normal day strenuous and causing me to breathe heavily. This was not the flu, but what was it? It was like I was having a panic attack, where I'd struggle for air, not get enough, and need to take bigger and bigger breaths to try to get enough oxygen in. With all my previous physical training and healthy eating, these problems shouldn't be. This was not good, and I was really getting worried, as was my husband at the time.

    I have to give tremendous credit to my first husband, as he was my biggest advocate, fighting to ensure the doctors understood I wasn't well. He came to every appointment, researched illness after illness, insisted that the doctors investigate until we got answers, and always believed me when I explained how I felt. He made sure I didn't feel like it was all just in my head. My doctor also never gave up the search until we finally knew what was going on. She also made me feel sane, and that something really was wrong.

What is Going On?

Now, as a nurse, all sorts of possibilities were running through my head at this point. My biggest concern was my breathing, as that is the symptom that came first, and presented out of nowhere. There are three main systems responsible for breathing, the lungs, heart, and brain.

`The logical place to start was to examine my lungs. As the distress in my breathing was of sudden onset, and because of the clot that resulted in my stroke years prior, both my doctor and I worried that a clot got to my lungs, and I could be suffering from a pulmonary embolism. This resulted in a direct trip to emergency to be assessed for this life-threatening condition. Thankfully, I was cleared of any clots in my lungs being the cause and I was then set up with a pulmonary function test. This determined how well my lungs worked in their ability to take in and transfer oxygen to the rest of my body. This assessment also came back clear. So, if my lungs are working properly, why can't I breathe?

The next place to look was at my heart, as there are many heart conditions that affect a person's ability to breathe. I underwent a series of heart assessments, ultimately clearing that from contributing to my shortness of breath. Okay, so now two out of three systems were cleared, leaving my brain to be next on the list to check.

By this time, I had developed weakness in my limbs, and couldn't even walk up a flight of stairs without requiring a break. The home care office was located on the second floor, and I used to always take the stairs without breaking stride, now I was taking the elevator, at 37 years of age. I felt ridiculous, but I didn't have a choice. Things were getting complicated, and it wasn't only my breathing that was of concern, so more tests were added.

A CAT scan was scheduled to take images of my brain, looking for possible tumors, clots, swelling, and overall neurological functioning. This would also indicate if Multiple Sclerosis was the cause, which was our growing question at the time given the results of the previous tests and my growing physical weakness. It came back clear as a bell. I also had a neurological assessment to determine if there was a disconnect between the signals from my brain and the muscles they controlled. Again, not the cause of my problems.

Over the period of June to February, I was sent to specialist after specialist to rule out every possible disease and illness. I underwent bloodwork for everything you could imagine, all coming back negative. Not only did we have no diagnosis yet, but my condition worsened.

As I already stated, my breathing was strained, and I was growing weaker and weaker. Over time, my memory became clouded, as did my judgement. I had delayed reactions, my limbs felt like they were 300 pounds, and I felt like a zombie. By the end of the day, I couldn't think, couldn't formulate a response to a simple question, and stared blankly when I was spoken to. I had to crawl up the stairs to my bedroom, and once upstairs, I couldn't make it back down. My then husband was now shouldering all the responsibilities at home, and I was an empty shell. We didn't know yet, that all these symptoms meant anything. It was in hindsight that we later understood that these were classic attributes of ME/CFS. I simply attributed it all to putting in a long day at work.

In the mornings, however, it was the weakness that was the persistent factor, so I continued to work despite these issues. My job didn't require much of me physically, so I diligently continued to show up to work every day. I didn't think I had a good enough reason to take time off, as I could do my job, I just couldn't function afterwards.

Okay, I'm Not Fine

February 2, 2014 was the last day I ever worked as a nurse. On that particular morning, despite taking the elevator as I had been doing for months, my legs gave out from under me, and I nearly hit the ground. Thankfully, I was near the wall, and leaned up against it instead. After some time, I managed to make my way to my desk where I sat, exhausted by the effort of getting there. This was the first time I realized I wasn't okay, like really not okay. I seriously had to reassess my situation.

    I was no longer safe to work, not only for myself physically, but I came to the realization that I wasn't safe for my clients, either. I couldn't trust myself to safely assess, let alone provide the care my clients deserved. Given my delayed reaction time, I was also unfit to drive. I'd see a light turn yellow, my brain would register that I needed to apply the brakes, but my foot wouldn't leave the gas pedal. I couldn't provide the quality of care I wanted, and needed to, for my clients. This broke my heart and was ultimately why I went on medical leave in the hopes of soon returning.

    Talk about not listening to what my body was trying to tell me. It wasn't the dismal state of health I was in that was the determining factor for whether I continued to work or not, it was the fact that I literally could no longer do my job. I had hit the wall and couldn't deny it any longer. My body was forcing me to stop and rest, regardless of the fact that I didn't want to. It was later said by a colleague that they saw it coming for months, yet I couldn't see it coming myself.

Queen Bee

    I'm a doer, very independent, and before I got sick, I tended to mind the household operations, etc. as my then husband worked twelve-hour shifts and I had the time to do it. I also liked to do it. When people offered to help, I'd refuse, as it was usually easier for me to do it myself, versus explaining what needed to be done. Now, I found myself in a very awkward and uncomfortable position of having to rely on others for everything. I felt like a queen bee, resting in my chair, asking for this or that because I couldn't get it myself. I felt like such a burden to my family, and I had to put my ego aside, swallow my pride, and ask for the help. This did not come naturally to me, and I really struggled with having to do so. I mean, from the outside looking in, I would've appeared to be the laziest, bossiest person around, and that ate at me. I did it because I had to, but that didn't matter. It felt lazy to me, and I despised myself for it. I hated to not be able to do things for myself and felt I made things harder on everyone around me.

I will always be grateful to my first husband for all he found himself having to take on amidst working full time shift work. He took care of the cooking, cleaning, kids, and me. The kids would lend a hand where they could, but he carried the load. Our household was a lot for two adults to manage, let alone one, but he did it, somehow.

But my illness took a toll on him, and the kids as well. The stress and having to deal with my ever-changing condition was a lot for us all. Everyone was starting to get burned out and we were struggling to do it all ourselves. But my family simply did what had to be done and that was the was we existed.

I'm Losing Everything

I'd always wanted to be a nurse, and after thirty years, I had become one. I spent a blissful eight years happily going to work every shift, and now it was all over. I had no idea what to do with myself, nor did I know who I was. I'd formed my identity around being a nurse, and I'd lost not only my occupation, my passion, but also myself. Who was I, if not Erin, the nurse? Nursing was my outlet to the adult world. It was how I interacted with the world, how I contributed to it. Now I found myself unable to participate in the world, as I had become so debilitated, I couldn't leave my home. I lost the thing that brought me joy, working with others and helping them heal.

I also found I'd lost my friends. Many of these friends were work friends. This didn't happen over night, but over a series of months, friends stopped checking in on me, stopped coming around. I mean, I understood, people are busy, life happens, I couldn't go to them or give back in any meaningful way, and there's a lot to be said for out of sight, out of mind. I kept in contact with a rare few people online, but even that dwindled as time went on. It's difficult to have a conversation with someone when your side of it boils down to "I'm still sick, we don't know how to fix it, and I haven't been out of the house in months." It's a pretty one-sided interaction, and I don't blame anyone for fading away.

Without being able to interact in the outside world, I fell behind on what people were doing, how their lives were changing, when before, I would be aware of such things and carry on a relevant conversation with people. It was a very lonely time, that's for certain, especially as I love interacting with others. I just didn't have the energy to be able to leave the house. If I did venture out, it was in a wheelchair, and it would take days to recover from the exertion. So, in essence, I'd also lost my freedom.

    At the same time as everything else was fading away, my symptoms kept on coming. I still had all the previously mentioned ailments, but the worst was about to come. ME/CFS affects all sorts of systems within the body, even if we don't know exactly how yet. For me, I was coping with the extreme fatigue, the lack of mobility, the fuzzy brain, and such, but I absolutely could not handle it when my senses became hyperactive. It was completely unbearable. I was unable to watch TV or look at anything moving, as my eyes couldn't keep up with the movement and I would get dizzy. I had noise cancelling headphones as everything, even a whisper, was too loud. And the worst of it all was the sensations on my skin. It was so sensitive that my skin felt like it was on fire. The mere movement of air hurt. Imagine not being able to hug your children without it causing physical pain. Not only did it hurt physically, but it hurt my heart as well.

    My family tiptoed around me, had to talk in whispers, treat me like a fragile leaf that could shatter at any moment. They couldn't live normal, active lives around me, and had to essentially treat me like a paper doll. We missed out on talks, snuggles, outings, quality family time, and it was my fault. Not only was my life miserable, but my then husband and the kids suffered too. It was heartbreaking to see how much my family was losing out on.

My Life is Over

My world was not so suddenly crashing down around me. The life I had was over. I was no longer a nurse, which gave me an identity, and I couldn't function as a spouse or mother in any way I felt was meaningful. I didn't know who I was without my work. It was what had defined me for eight years and I took tremendous pride in providing care to others.

By this time, I had seen all the specialists, all ruling out the illnesses that fell under their expertise, and we had concluded that the likelihood was that I did, in fact have ME/CFS, but we didn't have a way to know for sure until I could get an appointment with the one psychiatrist in Alberta who assessed for it. It was the one last chance we had at putting a name to the symptoms and perhaps get some help in alleviating them.

As days passed, my symptoms got worse and worse, and I had a terrible time adjusting. I was legitimately an invalid, barely able to walk the short 15 steps from my chair to the bathroom. I couldn't cook, clean, or contribute to a discussion. Not only was my physical health in dire straits, my mental capacity was nil. My brain was literally empty. I had no thoughts forming in my head.

At the height of my illness, I spent months laying in bed, in a dark room, with ear plugs in to dampen any sounds, the sheets hurting my skin. The sound of my heartbeat and my own breathing were all that kept me company. My family tiptoed around me so as not to disturb me, and I would wince in pain when my children would come and hug me goodnight. Once again, I found myself at the mercy of a body that was failing me, more so than ever. I felt like a ghost in the house, there but not really there.

Again, I wasn't paying attention to what the Universe was trying to tell me. I needed to nurture myself and take care of not only my body, but my soul. It was time to stop repressing my feelings and emotions like I conditioned myself to do. I was overwhelmed by all that I hadn't ever dealt with. My body was literally shutting down so that I could do the internal healing I needed to do, but I didn't realize it at that point, let alone know how to do it. So my physical symptoms only got worse. This then led to my mental and emotional state crumbling.

Chapter Eight: The Darkness

Did you know that approximately 1.9 million, or 26% of North Americans suffer from depression at any given time? Now, the caveat to this is that these are reported cases and do not account for the estimated millions of undiagnosed or untreated individuals affected by this illness. It is also important to note most people will be affected by some form of depression at least once in their lives, if not more so. How's that, you may ask? How does that relate to the statistics? Well, there are three factors to consider. First, the statistics are for at any given time. Second, there is the undiagnosed population. And third, there are two main categories of depression. Let me go into those a little further now.

What most people understand as depression is medically known as Major Depressive Disorder (MDD), which presents as long term, chronic depression. It is often difficult to treat depending on its severity, but therapies include medications, counselling, self care routines, and electromagnetic stimulation therapy, to name a few. The goal is to stimulate serotonin production and maintain a steady supply of it in the brain to improve neurological functioning. This form of the illness is lifelong. I've been medicated for MDD since I was 21, but looking back now, it was more a series of situational depression, anxiety, and another mental illness that I'll discuss shortly.

The second type of depression I'd like to mention is Situational Depression. This form of depression is the result of a specific trigger and is temporary. On average, it lasts at most, two years. It has the same symptoms of depression but can be overcome. Oftentimes, medication is prescribed for a short period of time until the person can adopt the coping skills to get through the depressive episode. A common trigger for Situational Depression is the death of a loved one. The grief and overwhelm leads to a depression that can be difficult to cope with, but through therapies and time, resolves itself. People can go through several bouts of Situational Depression in their lifetime, but the key difference is the duration and the fact that it is, for lack of a better word, curable.

As we have become more aware of depression and its prominence in our society, other forms of the illness have also been identified. Aside from the two previously mentioned, the five other most common forms are Bipolar Disorder which is lifelong, Postpartum Depression, Atypical Depression (MDD in which certain situations can bring you happiness), Premenstrual Dysphoric Disorder, and Seasonal Affective Disorder. Aside from the depressions elaborated on, these forms are situational, yet lifelong. By no means should "situational" diminish the validity or intensity of the symptoms associated with any, and all, of the above, as they are very real.

Now that I've discussed types of depression, I'd like to touch on the some of the typical symptoms one might experience. By no means is this an exhaustive list, and the intensity and combinations of symptoms vary from person to person, episode to episode, and even from day to day. The National Institute for Mental Health currently lists persistent episodes of sadness, anxiety, or "emptiness", hopelessness, helplessness, irritability, worthlessness, loss of interest, fatigue, concentration issues, physical aches, pains, and digestive issues, and suicidal tendencies, to name a few. Again, this is just a summary, and subjective to each individual case.

    Depression affects the lives of so many, and the number of people suffering in silence is heartbreaking. Even though there have been major strides to bring awareness to the reality of depression and to destigmatize it, we have a long way to go to eliminate the shame people still feel for suffering from it. Not only does it affect the depressed person, but the people around them as well. Here is my story of battling with depression…

The Spiral

    I've been on antidepressants since I was 21, but I'm certain I had bouts of depression long before becoming medicated. For example, I lost a very dear family friend, a man I called uncle, when I was in grade nine. It was sudden, and I didn't go to the funeral for the sake of a boy at school. From that day, and for the next year and a half, I broke out in terrible hives constantly. After a battle of tests, it was determined it was an emotional response from not dealing with my grief and loss. Remember how I spoke of our bodies creating ailments or illnesses when we suppress our emotions? Here is yet another example of my body doing just that. My body was trying to tell me to go within and deal with that pain. Between the bullying during my school years and this, my first significant loss, I'd no doubt been depressed then. I can see, looking back now, and knowing what I know, that I was depressed for years.

I suppose that as I reflect on when I was first medicated, I was struggling with anxiety, more than depression. I was engaged and planning my first wedding, doing everything myself as I'm OCD and was a control freak. I was put on antidepressants as I was losing my mind over the smallest of things. It was the oddest thing, as I knew I was overreacting, yet my mind wouldn't shut the freak outs down even when I wanted it to. It was like an out of body experience, watching the melt down yet unable to stop it. So Celexa was the first antidepressant I was given by my general practitioner, and it worked well enough at the time.

As I had children, especially once they were born, my medication was increased to balance out the depression and anxiety that was likely postpartum depression, but that was never actually written in my charts. Thankfully my doctors were proactive so that I only had mild cases of depression during those times and functioned well.

I was stable for years with Celexa and didn't even get depressed when I had my stroke. I feel that would've been very different if I hadn't recovered as quickly and as well as I did. When Chronic Fatigue Syndrome came into play, now that was an entirely different story. As more physical symptoms arose, resulting in limitations on my abilities and ultimately having to leave my dream job, depression hit, and it hit hard.

It began as a slowly progressing sadness that I couldn't seem to shake. As the pieces of my life seemed to be taken away one at a time, the depression grew. The losses were coming faster than I could keep up with, and so was the guilt of not being able to contribute to my family in any meaningful way. My husband at the time was very supportive, and insisted that me just being there was enough, but I couldn't believe him. I simply felt like a burden to everyone. This was especially the case when I became bed-ridden and unable to do anything for myself. That was when the depression really took over.

Medication Upgrade

The reason for addressing medications here is that antidepressants, amongst other medications, must be considered carefully and monitored diligently when being prescribed for the first time, or when changes are made as the side effects can be dangerous. For example, depression can become worse before the medication takes full effect, which typically takes six to eight weeks. Suicidal thoughts and tendencies are another extreme, but not an uncommon, side effect. Scary, but true.

As my physician who'd been the lead in figuring out my ME/CFS became aware of my decline, she decided to switch me from Celexa, an SSRI to Cymbalta, an SNRI, a much newer and more effective antidepressant. After all, it had been at least fifteen years since I'd first started with Celexa. Cymbalta worked on two neural pathways as opposed to only the one that Celexa did. SSRIs prevented the reuptake of serotonin in the brain, so there is more of it hanging around during neural processing. SNRIs did this, but also prevented norepinephrine from reuptake as well, further improving neural functioning. The most important thing is that serotonin and norepinephrine are the chemicals that affect our mood, they are the happiness chemicals in our brain. When we are depressed, these chemicals are diminished and medications help replace them.

For me, it was time for an upgrade, and Cymbalta helped me overcome the overwhelm, for the most part. It was definitely more effective than the Celexa had been. I also had to give the process time and have patience as we slowly decreased the Celexa and introduced Cymbalta to my system. Thankfully, the transition was a positive one, and went smoothly. No major side effects were noted except for the minor inconvenience of muscle twitches that randomly caught me by surprise. It was more amusing than a problem, and certainly worth dealing with as my mood did, in fact, improve… for a time, that is.

What Quality of Life?

So, to recap, my body was declining and my depression was on the rise. I'd been through all the tests and examinations I could possibly go through. I'd spent about nine months lounging on the reclining chaise in the living room day after day, my only trips were to the bathroom and back, thirty steps... fifteen there, and fifteen back. My family members brought me everything I needed otherwise. At the end of the day, it would literally take all the strength I had to climb the stairs to my bedroom. I would have to sit down every few steps and take a break, and by the time I reached the top of the stairs, I was out of breath and in a full sweat. I would sit to brush my teeth because I couldn't tolerate standing, then be in bed for the night.

Herein lied the rub. Chronic Fatigue Syndrome affects the adrenaline cycle. It bypasses the adrenaline off switch, resulting in being extremely tired, but wired at the same time. Imagine being so exhausted that breathing felt difficult, yet your heart was racing and you felt like you just experienced the biggest rush of your life... At. The. Same. Time. Sleep was often difficult for me in the past, as my mind didn't want to shut off, but this was like nothing I'd ever dealt with before. So not only was I physically maxed out and exhausted, I couldn't sleep because the adrenaline was rushing though me like I'd just run a marathon. I'd be awake for days on end because I couldn't sleep. The typical sleeping pill was prescribed, Zopiclone being the one. But unfortunately, they were only effective part of the time.

As sleep is the number one factor needed for someone with ME/CFS to function, the lack of sleep further added to my decline. At this point I was now in bed full time, unable to get myself up as I was so weak and had become hypersensitive to everything. My ex-husband would bring me meals to the room and the kids would come hug me good night, but otherwise, I would lay in a dark, silent room. This lasted for several months, and as you could imagine, my mental and emotional state were greatly affected.

I felt useless, a burden to my family. I felt like a ghost in the house, there but not there. I felt it was unfair to my then partner to work full time shift work and care for me and the kids the rest of the time. I felt it wasn't fair to the kids to have to care for me and tiptoe around me because I couldn't tolerate anything more. I was an absent part of the family. There was no cure, just symptom control, and my symptoms had no management for them.

I was 38 years old, and this was not a life I wanted to lead. There was no quality of life at this point, laying motionless in bed, suffering with the mere sound of my breath and the beating of my heart as the only things I listened to moment after moment, hour after hour, day after day. As a nurse, we pay a lot of attention to optimizing a person's quality of life, especially as people become older, sicker, etc. We do all we can to compensate for what they lack and provide the highest quality of care to uphold the person's dignity and respect. But there was nothing anyone could do to help me. They couldn't make the symptoms go away, they couldn't make me better, and I couldn't take it anymore. I felt like I was ninety years old, existing but certainly not living. Forgotten about by life.

Dark Night- Part One

The darkest day I have ever had was Sunday, February 19, 2017, and it was the Family Day long weekend. My then husband was working a day shift, so I managed to make my way downstairs to be in the vicinity of our children. I had noise-canceling headphones on, and the boys were playing with Lego and coloring, and spending the day doing relatively calm activities, while I laid on our chaise lounge.

That day was a day that my mind got the better of me, running amok with all the thoughts of how useless I was, how much of a burden I was to my family, how much I felt invisible, a ghost. And I broke down… hard. The uncontrollable sobbing began early afternoon, racking my body so heavily I couldn't breathe. My husband at the time texted to check in on me as he often did when he was working, and I briefly texted back how I felt. This alarmed him enough that he phoned me to check on both myself and the kids, and I could barely utter any words as the sobs controlled me.

Over the course of the afternoon, I'd decided I had had enough of this world, and that everyone would be better off without me burdening them. Yes, there would be a brief period of sadness, but then my loved ones could move on without me weighing them down. I didn't say anything that day, I just continued to be in a nearly catatonic state, shut down from the world around me, the only thing I could do was cry, cry until I had no tears left, just the sobbing.

When my first husband arrived home, he just came and held me, held me as I was curled up in a little ball, the only comfort anyone could provide as I continued to have my breakdown. I cried, and cried, until I could cry no more. He whispered words of support, and he also made me aware that the kids were scared and didn't know how to make me feel better. I was so stuck in my own head that I was oblivious to what was going on around me, and how I was affecting the boys. But I couldn't shake it. I was in the throes of a breakdown so deep, there was no getting out of it. I didn't eat, didn't move from the fetal position I was in, didn't speak, I just sobbed like never before.

Finally, at some point in the evening, my ex-husband helped me upstairs to our bedroom so I could get some rest, the sobbing seeming to have past for the time being. This is when I was able to solidify my plan to leave this world behind. I'd take all the sleeping pills I had, have the boys and my then husband snuggling with me in our king size bed, and peacefully fall asleep for good. I'd be able to tell my children how much I loved them, and leave this world surrounded by the ones I loved most. Unlike when I had my stroke, now I was ready to go, and I had made my peace with it.

When my then husband came to bed after putting the kids down, he had in his hands pictures the boys had colored for me, to cheer me up. I have those pictures with me to this day. Finally, I was able to speak, and I told him all about how I didn't want to be here anymore, that everyone would be better off with me gone. This was explained very rationally, this was not a ploy for sympathy, this was carefully thought out and rationalized.

Rational suicide is a real thing. It is defined by one taking their own life based on logical decision making. This was what I had done, where I was at, and my decision made clear sense. As a nurse, I'd been a part of other people's end of life, I saw the many different ways people left this world. And I saw how many people wanted to be able to do it on their own terms. I felt this wholly and completely. My life wasn't a life, it was only an existence. I couldn't fathom another forty or fifty years of living as a ghost, trapping my family in the misery with me. It was time for me to go.

My husband at the time and I spoke for hours about how I felt it was my right to choose, and that I didn't want to live anymore, him countering all my points with points of his own, also rational but in contrast to mine. The problem was that he couldn't feel how I felt physically, mentally, or emotionally, although he tried. He understood how I felt like I didn't exist and insisted that I was loved and truly did exist. But in my eyes, it wasn't enough. After the most intimate and emotionally draining conversation we had ever had, he fell asleep, exhausted and believing we had resolved things.

    Well, I didn't fall asleep despite my exhaustion. I was finalizing my plans. I realized I couldn't do it the way I had envisioned that night, as the boys were already asleep, and their dad wouldn't allow them to ever witness their mother take her own life. I had to wait until the next day so that I could at least talk to each of them, letting them know how much I loved them, pass on some words of wisdom, and say my goodbyes. Then I could do what I needed to do.

    For me, I didn't want to suffer, and I didn't want to traumatize whoever it was that found me by doing something violent, so I chose pills. I wanted to be sure that the pills did the job and did it right. So, I went to my medicine box and counted out the Zopiclone I had on hand. There were 95 sky blue pills. I know because I sat on the bathroom floor and counted them. That ought to be enough to do the trick, right? I looked at their medicinal properties and warnings, pulled out my nursing drug book and researched them, and searched them on the internet. Then a niggle of a thought made its way from the back of my mind to the forefront. Somehow, from somewhere, I recalled that sleeping pills don't actually succeed in ending a person's life, they only add to the strife because they damage organs and create even worse health problems, exactly what I wanted to avoid. This was a dilemma, because I wasn't going to end my life any other way, and it was a one time shot, I definitely didn't want to mess it up. I was going to do it right, or I wasn't going to do it at all.

And so, the racking sobs began again as I realized my plan wouldn't work. I didn't have any other options, and I couldn't fathom living life the way it was. I returned the pills to their container, put the medicine box away, and returned to bed, crying my eyes out. My first husband woke up to my sobbing and asked what was wrong. I explained all about my plan and how devastated I was to realize it wasn't going to work. After such an emotionally draining day, I finally cried myself to sleep.

When I awoke the next day, I found my then husband on the phone with my sister, also a nurse, strategizing about what to do. This was a holiday Monday, remember, so seeing my doctor was not an option that day. He had removed all the medications from our bathroom, and everywhere else in the house while I was asleep, and took that day, and the next few days off work to be able to watch out for me. At this point, I had given up on the plan since it would have failed. But I was to see my doctor the following morning and had to make a promise to both my ex-husband and my sister that if I was feeling like suicidal again, that I was to reach out to them no matter what time of day or night. I promised, but knew I wasn't likely to follow through with calling my sister as she had five kids of her own and a full-time job. She didn't need me adding to her already busy life with my problems. I would be honest and forthcoming with my partner, however.

I had already given up on my plan as the logistics of it didn't work, so I was resigned to accepting that I had to live as I was. It was utterly disappointing, but it was what it was. The day was a quiet one, as neither of us slept much, and there was a lot of worry remaining even though I had accepted my fate and let my ex-husband know I had no more intentions of taking my life. We got through the day, did a lot of talking about plans and how to support me, spent time with the boys, and I was agreeable to all the steps he had put into place.

The next morning, I saw my doctor and went through the whole situation with her, start to finish. We all agreed that I was to come in weekly to assess how I was doing, my antidepressants were increased, and I had to promise to give it until I saw the psychiatrist who was the only person in Alberta to assess me formally for ME/CFS before making any rash decisions. I accepted all the conditions and took it one day at a time until the psychiatrist appointment. The days weren't easy, but I was holding onto the hope that answers and help would come, I just had to be patient and get through each day. I didn't really have any better options, anyhow.

At the end of June 2017, was when I was assessed, and subsequently diagnosed with Chronic Fatigue Syndrome. Now I had hope, as the psychiatrist gave a list of recommendations for coping with my syndrome and the symptoms associated with it. We were so excited for new things to try and have a clearer direction moving forward. Perhaps I could have a somewhat normal life with all these new plans and suggestions from the ME/CFS expert.

Dark Night- Part Two

Life was going pretty smoothly following my assessment and diagnosis of Chronic Fatigue Syndrome. There was hope in the air, and I began to implement some of the recommendations from the specialist. One of those suggestions was to reduce the number of medications I was on, as she felt they were ineffectively treating my depression and sleep issues. So, under supervision of my family doctor, I began to carefully wean off the Cymbalta and Zopiclone and try an alternative therapy. This spoke to my first husband and I as I didn't like being on medications if I could help it anyhow.

The alternative therapy was to introduce CBD oil for anxiety during the day and THC oil for sleep during the night. Getting past the texture of the oil took some getting used to, but I managed. The THC oil only lasted about three days, as I very much did not like the feeling of not being in control that came with it. I didn't like the "high" no matter how little it was. I took the CBD oil religiously, however.

Over the course of July and August, I had to increase the oil from 1ml three times a day to 3ml three times a day. Again, all this was done in consultation with the licensed medical marijuana specialists. By this time, the texture of the oil was something my body was not liking and would produce a gag effect when I took it. Luckily, drinking some juice or other beverage right after helped.

In regards to how my anxiety and depression were responding to this new therapy, was somewhat difficult to tell. I did have to increase the initial dose to feel better, but I also felt that it could work, given the time to adjust to it. Sleeping was a different matter. And lack of sleep directly corresponded to how my day would go.

I was learning how to monitor my energy output, and the effects it had on my fatigue. The difficulty there was that something I overdid three days ago could be the cause of fatigue half a week later. I also had to learn to rest even on the good days, as I would do more on those days because I felt better, but then end up in a worse state of fatigue the next few days because I did too much. It was a lot of trial and error, and a lot of guesswork. Thankfully my ex-husband was very supportive and great at reminding me to watch my energy output. I hoped the oil would assist in the hypersensitivities, and through trial and error, we found ways to help, at least a little bit. Noise cancelling headphones were a huge saving grace, which helped with one of the most overwhelming symptoms, only surpassed by that of being physically sensitive.

Things were now at a turning point. I was in a relatively even mood most of the time, I seemed to handle the anxiety alright, and I was feeling less overwhelmed, but not to the degree that I was before, or that I needed, or wanted, to be. I felt okay, but certainly not my best. At this point, I had maxed out the CBD dosage at 5ml three times a day, and we were facing making the switch to a different strain of CBD oil or going back to medications. Ultimately, we opted to return to medical intervention, and Trintillex, another newer SNRI was introduced in the middle of August. Again, there was the six-to-eight-week period where it takes the medication to reach its full effect, but I was being monitored weekly, and was patient with the process.

During this time, I don't remember feeling depressed. I was disappointed that I had to return to prescription medications but made my peace with it as some people just need to do so. I was one of those people. I do know I wasn't at my best yet, but believed it was just a matter of time before I would be. I just needed to wait for the medication to take effect.

As it turns out, I wasn't as well as I thought I was. The depression and anxiety got worse before they got better, and I was trying to be patient and allow the Trintillex to do its thing, but my mental health was declining. While I was waiting for full effect of the medication, I became rather fixated on the thought of suicide again. Not that I had a set plan like I did in February, but I was no longer limited to the idea of pills being the only route I'd consider. As a nurse, I was also curious why people chose to cut their wrists as opposed to other more major vessels. Was it that this was easy? Was it just that it was common? Was it difficult to access other arteries? So, I tried to do a little research, but was stymied by the fact that I really am poor at navigating search engines.

I began to voice these thoughts to my then husband, who became concerned. Who could blame him? He debated taking time off work and arranging other supports to stay with me to ensure my safety. I confess I was a little worried myself that I was thinking this way. I mean, I wasn't planning to act upon anything, but I certainly had several plans formulating in my head. As he was trying to come up with ways to keep me safe, I said something that changed the course of everything.

I'd said that the reality was that if I was determined to end my life, nothing and nobody could realistically stop me. This stopped him dead in his tracks and he made a phone call to my sister, the nurse, who knew how to navigate the mental health system. When the phone call ended, I was instructed to pack a bag as we were going to the hospital… now.

So, I did as I was told and packed a bag, all the while not thinking that the hospital would do anything but send me home as I wasn't acting on my plans, I just had them in my head. Little did I know. My first husband was directed on what to say at the hospital, the key phrase was that he could not keep me safe. When I was interviewed, I didn't deny my thoughts or the fact that I had considered taking my life before. I expected that to be the end of that, and we would go back home.

Nope. Instead, I was admitted to the University of Alberta Hospital emergency psychiatric unit. Here, I was further assessed, and it was determined that I was going to be held there until a bed opened in a psychiatric unit in one of Edmonton's hospitals. It was intimidating to be in this emergency ward. My belongings were locked up, anything with a cord was sent home with my then husband, and I was scared. There were patients here with all sorts of mental health issues, it was loud, people were unpredictable, and it was overwhelming. I was there for two days, with little sleep to go on, until there was an opening for me. All things considered, it was a short wait, and I was grateful for that.

 Just as my family was coming in to visit with me, the ambulance arrived to transfer me to the Grey Nuns Hospital. The boys were timid, seeing me in a hospital gown and then being ushered to an ambulance, but were a little better after we explained that the doctors had to watch me while my medicine started to work, and were even more reassured seeing that I wasn't physically sick. It helped that the ambulance attendants were very patient and understanding, giving the boys a tour of the ambulance and explaining what everything was. Then it was time for me to go, as we were on a timeline. I gave the boys huge hugs and kisses, not knowing when I'd see them next as this was foreign territory for me and I was given only a brief outline of what to expect. It was unclear until the admitting doctor assessed me at the new hospital as to when I would be permitted to speak to my family. It all depended on what they felt was safe.

Unit 91

Arriving at the Grey Nuns Unit 91 at 7:30 pm was an eerie experience. There was a lone nurse awaiting my arrival, and nobody else around. It was so quiet, I wondered if anyone else was even there. It was further intimidating in that it was made very clear that I'd be responsible for getting around on my own, something that I hadn't been able to do to the degree that was expected of me for years. My entire body convulsed as I laid on my bed, the nurse describing the expectations and asking me all the questions about mood, suicidal thoughts, depression, etc. I had no idea how I was going to do this, the physical component, that is. I could barely get to the bathroom and back, let alone to the meeting rooms and appointments I was to attend. I was snapped out of this train of thought when the nurse went through all my belongings. Anything with a cord, my floss, tweezers, and nail clippers were confiscated as they were a hazard. It didn't even occur to me that floss or tweezers could be considered a weapon, but I was, after all, in a psychiatric unit for suicidal thoughts, and I wasn't the only one there for the same thing. Then I was left to get settled with the remainder of my things and would have to wait until the following day to do the official intake with the psychiatrist. It was a difficult night as I wasn't permitted my medications until the psychiatrist okayed them, so sleep was fleeting.

In the morning, everyone was expected to be up for 8 am breakfast. This was another thing that was going to take getting used to as I tended to sleep until late morning. My non-dairy and non-grain diet was not able to be accommodated, another adjustment, but I felt deep within me that I was where I needed to be. Just before noon, the doctor assigned to me arrived and we talked about why and how I came to be there. He seemed very focussed on my depression, but I didn't feel he understood that the depression was a direct result of the Chronic Fatigue Syndrome, which for me, was the biggest factor. It felt like I wasn't being fully heard, as the depression was the only thing the psychiatrist seemed interested in treating. At least he prescribed sleeping medications so I could get a proper rest, as this was one of the most important issues that needed to be resolved.

Over the course of the next few days, I started to settle into the routine of the Unit and was told the fact that I was to expect to be there for at least four weeks. If memory serves, I believe it was the fourth day when the psychiatrist realized that the Chronic Fatigue Syndrome needed to be addressed. This was the day my life changed forever because this was the day that he introduced two medications into my regimen specifically targeting the worst of my symptoms. Abilify was prescribed to increase my energy, and Fetzima tamed the hypersensitivities. My symptoms went away within two days! I was in disbelief… for so long I was of the understanding that there was nothing I could do about the things that drove me to the brink of ending my life, and in a matter of only two days, I could function! The Universe was looking out for me, that's for sure.

After the first week, I was granted supervised weekends at home, and then unsupervised ones. I fully participated in all the courses and sessions and was a model patient. I'm a social creature at heart, so I quickly made friends with the other patients. We'd play card games, color, and assemble puzzles in the common areas, and go for coffee together when granted passes from the unit. This is where my journey with journaling began. At first, I had no idea what the hell I was doing, and it was mostly just a rundown of the things I did each day. It took a while, but over time, I began to write out my feelings or work through questions I had going on in my head. Soon, I didn't go anywhere without my journal. This way of connecting with myself was one of the biggest take-aways from my time in the hospital.

I spent a total of four weeks in Unit 91 and was recommended for a six-week outpatient program, building on the tools and teachings that began in the unit sessions. I was eager to attend these, as I was absorbing the information like a sponge and wanted to learn everything I possibly could. As an added bonus, my favorite friend from the unit was in this course as well. We'd both arrive early each day and settle in with our coffees in hand, waiting for class to begin. As I did as a student in the unit, I was a stellar student during this six-week program and was subsequently referred to the twelve-week outpatient program by the therapists running them.

This twelve-week program was intense, but worth it. It was a deep dive into all sorts of issues, taught me a language to describe my emotions, dug into childhood issues, unresolved traumas, you name it. But no matter how much I invested myself into the homework and assignments, the feedback from the therapists was that I was holding back, not digging deep enough. I didn't know how to dig deeper, I felt I was digging as deeply as I possibly could. It bothered me that it was possible that I wasn't getting as much out of the program as I could be if I could connect with a deeper level of emotions, so I sat down with the lead psychiatrist running the course to discuss it. This meeting was yet another life-changing moment, as she revealed a startling diagnosis, but one that rang truer than anything I'd heard before, and so much more of my life began to make sense.

Chapter Nine: Borderline Personality Disorder

    Many people are not for labels or diagnoses, and that's perfectly fine by me. I, on the other hand, appreciate them, not as a label, but as an understanding of what makes me who I am. For example, I am not my stroke, Chronic Fatigue Syndrome, nor am I Borderline Personality Disorder (BPD), but all of those diagnoses are a real part of who I am. BPD was an especially important diagnosis as I'd gone around for years, from adolescence, with a combination of seemingly random symptoms or issues, which, when properly diagnosed with Borderline Personality Disorder, all made sense because instead of being random, they were, in fact, a part of a whole.

Oooooohhh, That Makes Sense

    I had wondered for years why I felt, or didn't feel, certain things, why I thought the way I did, and why I didn't understand things the way most people did. The truth of the matter is that my brain is actually wired differently. There are areas that don't function as fully as others, and some areas that are bypassed altogether. A few of the main symptoms of BPD are impulsiveness, unstable emotions which are difficult to regulate, lack of feeling/dulled emotions, and a distorted self-image. Well, this was me, to a tee. This was why, when prescribed antidepressants at 21, they had some effect.

Some people would have been horrified or devastated to receive such a diagnosis, and rightfully so as it isn't fun. I however, felt relief. I now had a much clearer understanding of why I always felt differently and had the medical support to explain it. As I said earlier, I am not any of my diagnoses, but they do play a role in shaping who I am.

Haven't I Been Through Enough

There was a brief period of time where I felt sorry for myself. I wondered how much more the Universe was going to throw my way. I mean, I'd been through a lot of big things in my nearly forty years. This was yet another. Couldn't someone else shoulder this? Why did it have to be me? Borderline Personality Disorder can be lessened with medications and therapy, but the wiring of the brain that controls the scariest symptoms, the lack of emotions and the distorted self-image don't go away. Although everything now made sense, it didn't make things easier.

Great, So I Have No Feelings?

With understanding, can eventually come acceptance. Going back to the concerns of the counsellors in the twelve-week program, that I wasn't reaching the depth of emotions that they wanted me to, now made sense. My brain just wasn't wired that way. Frankly, I'd felt like a shitty human being for years... not connecting to my then husband, feeling the love that others felt. I didn't even feel it with my children. Think about that for a moment. These perfect little humans that you brought into the world, new parents crying with joy and love, and I didn't feel any differently with their arrival than if I'd just gotten groceries. Horrible, right? Of course I'd feel more than that, everyone does... but the reality is that wasn't true for me.

I have a dulled sense of emotions, good, bad, or ugly. It was really difficult not to take that personally. No wonder I felt like I lived like a ghost, because emotionally I was disconnected from everyone, whether I wanted to be or not. I certainly didn't choose to be so cut off, so removed emotionally from the people that meant the most to me, and I definitely don't wish that on anyone else. It's incredibly isolating, I felt broken, and I felt the loss of not being able to feel as fully as most people do. I grieved the inability to fully know what love was, and that I wasn't able to give to others what I wanted to.

I did have much to be grateful for. I was a high-functioning person with BPD, not self-harming like many. I was able to live my life with my diagnosis without it being a major disruption, and I tried to love as best as I could. My family still heard "I love you", got all the hugs, kisses, and I meant every word, I just didn't have the physical sensation of the emotion. I tried to make sure that they didn't lose out on my affection. I did, but at least I knew why and that it wasn't from a lack of trying.

    I have become so much more connected to myself since then. The work with coaches who were able to get be to those deeper places and learn how to connect with myself has brought me to a wonderful place. I still have BPD but I've led a fuller and richer life emotionally. I've been able to feel things I never thought I could, and I am so grateful!

Chapter Ten: The Chameleon

Life really began to make sense. Are you familiar with the chameleon? Think of Pascal from the Disney movie Tangled. It's the cool little lizard that changes colors to adapt to its surroundings. It is the chameleon's protective quality. Well, people use this adaptation, too. Without a solid sense of who I was as an individual, I lived my life chameleoning to fit in with the people around me. I didn't have my own opinions to voice, I echoed and agreed with the group I was with, even if it was contradictory to how I felt because of my deep desire to fit in. It was the people pleasing part of me at its best.

Really?! Me Too!

In elementary school to graduation, I'd chameleon by trying to remain invisible. I had tried to fit in to no avail, and I was with the same people throughout my entire school years, so hiding felt like it was my only option.

It was so much easier to go along with others then it was to think about, and actually have an opinion of my own. I could maneuver my way through conversations with just about anyone by the simple phrase, "me too." It was usually an instant in. That being said, I knew a little about a lot of things but didn't have depth to most of my knowledge. Except hockey. Hockey was, and is, something I know a lot about. But I digress.

As I really didn't know myself well enough to know what truly made me tick, I floated around from group to group, making small talk easily in all of them. When the group dissolved, however, so did the connection to others. This was after I started University, mind you. There were all sorts of different groups of people there, and I wandered through many of them seeking to fit in. I was excited that there were classmates and social groups who didn't shun me.

I'd make myself fit into friendships with classmates, coworkers, etc. after high school, as we had commonalities, but as time went by and these groups naturally dissolved, I never really had a strong enough friendship with anyone that lasted beyond the reason we were brought together in the first place. I would be remiss not to mention that this was a time before Facebook and other social media in which people could keep in touch even if they were half a world away.

What Opinion?

Being a chameleon also accommodated the way my brain was wired in that coming up with my own thoughts and ideas was a struggle. It was so much easier to go along with other people's ideas such as where to go for dinner or what to watch on TV. I do well when given a smaller selection to choose from as opposed to making a decision out of thin air. My brain literally goes blank in that situation.

    This came with downfalls, however. Not all suggestions were smart or safe ones. And I was an easy target for manipulation because I didn't tend to say no to things. I didn't always see the bigger picture of where a suggestion was leading and ended up in sticky situations on several occasions. Then it was especially difficult because I would be faced with then speaking up for myself and enforcing boundaries. This wasn't my strong suit until just a few years ago. Most often I would uncomfortably go along with whatever the situation was or try to sneak out of it. I am grateful to this day that I didn't experience worse.

    Not having boundaries in place for myself or for other people, not only affected me, but my ex-husband and children as well. I was inconsistent with what I would say and do and wasn't consistent with my parenting either. Chameleoning had me playing different characters at different times, and it confused everyone. Nobody knew which Erin was going to show up at any given time.

    I was not acting from a place of empowerment when I was chameleoning. In fact, I was giving my power away. Even in tiny decisions like deciding on dinner with my ex-husband or friends, I'd defer to them. I gave them the power to decide for me. This was no fault of theirs, and I don't mean to imply that they took advantage of me, I passively allowed others to choose when I could have spoken up for myself. Sometimes it really didn't matter to me which is why

Phoenix Rising

I'd let someone with a more invested interest in the outcome decide, but the times I did have an opinion and didn't share it are the times I gave my power away and usually had resentment about it. The resentment was towards myself, as I was the one who didn't stand in my power and speak my truth.

    Now knowing who I am, I no longer chameleon. I know what I want and speak my truth about it. I listen to my heart and allow it to guide me and take the necessary actions to follow through on a consistent basis. I don't try to fit in with or befriend everyone, I am simply me and I attract people into my life that are the right match for me. I have a small, intimate group of friends that I love dearly, and who accept me unconditionally.

Part Three

Stepping Into My Own

So, you may be asking where I'm at now... well I'm in a wonderful place. I've never felt more myself, my authentic self, without editing for others or people pleasing. I am comfortable in my own skin and feel like I am capable of anything. It has taken a lot of going within myself to discover who I truly am and, just as importantly, finding out who I am not.

I now live an empowered life, one that I am proud of, one that I make no explanations for, one that I make no excuses for, and one where I take ownership of all my decisions. After all, life is all about choices, even if at times we have to choose between a rock and a hard place, we still inevitably have to make a choice. Life is a series of choices, and we make them over and over. The key is awareness. When you're aware of patterns and habits, you can make conscious choices to improve your life. This is also where empowerment comes in as once you have the awareness, you can make different choices, empowered ones that move you forward in life. Now this is also where personal responsibility comes in and you need to hold yourself accountable for your choices, as once you become aware of your patterns, etc. you can't claim ignorance and that you didn't know better.

Phoenix Rising

    This is the part of my story that you've been waiting for. This is where I talk about the tangible action steps I've taken in order to create a better life for myself. Know that this isn't something you do once and all is cured, healing and growth is a life-long endeavor, and you'll have slips and stumbles, and have to get back up again. And that's okay! This is, and will forever be, a work in progress. In fact, that's what makes us human. I'm still a work in progress, and always will be.

Chapter Eleven: Breaking Toxic Patterns

During the past four years, the time I have really dedicated to working on myself, focussing on healing my inner wounds and growing, there were several main issues identified for me to work on especially. These patterns presented themselves throughout my life, and by addressing them, I was able to reclaim my personal power and truly live the life I desire. I speak to each of these patterns below.

External Validation

I spent a lifetime trying to seek validation for my achievements, and not just for me as a person, from others. Whether it was the praise of my parents, teachers, bosses, or friends, I had always sought fulfillment from external sources. Cue people pleasing to the extreme. I was an honors student, always followed the rules, and did all I could to be praised for my efforts. I sought praise for my actions, but what my heart really needed, I realize now, was that I was worthy for simply being. That I was good enough just as I was. Shockingly, no matter what I did or how perfect I tried to be, I never succeeded to feel fully validated.

Well, let me share with you the secret that I finally learned... you have to validate yourself. What is that, you say?! Yes! The answer to fulfillment is validating your own worth. It is up to you to be your

Phoenix Rising

own best cheerleader, your own best supporter, and to toot your own horn. You also have to be your own best friend. And, no, it isn't always easy, but this is the foundation to living the life that you want, because you truly know yourself, and aren't relying on others to fill a void.

You have value simply for existing and that is enough. You deserve to be loved and respected and cherished without being asked or expected to change. Recognizing this is fundamental in beginning to value yourself.

There are many techniques I used to break the pattern of looking outwards for validation. Personal mantras, positive affirmations about myself, helped to address my insecurities and turn my thoughts around. Positive self talk is another technique along the same lines of a mantra.

Again, this is something that takes practice, dedication, patience, and gentleness as you work on yourself. It isn't always easy to just be with yourself. It can be lonely, and I know for myself, I get antsy and seek interaction with others on a regular basis. But I have also grown comfortable spending time alone, dating myself, following what my heart wants, and learning to listen to my needs, not those of others. Balance is important, and now when I go to socialize, I do so because it makes my heart happy, not because I want someone else to impress anymore. I simply do me, enjoy my outings, and don't give a damn what others think.

Addictions

I've done a lot of work in terms of breaking addictions. There is a history of addiction on both sides of my family, alcoholism and smoking primarily. Knowing this, I likely have a predisposition to addiction, which makes it easier for me to fall into addictive tendencies.

There are all sorts of addictions out there. My addictions were to alcohol, smoking, shopping, binge eating, and male attention. Whether it be drugs, alcohol, shopping, over-eating, anything really, if it becomes a crutch or interferes with your life, then it is a problem. There's a difference between having a glass of wine to enjoy the experience and using the wine to numb yourself and avoid life, between buying a new pair of jeans because you wore out your favorite pair and spending a thousand dollars because you are upset. I think you probably get the idea.

It again, goes back to recognizing your own patterns. When you are aware of them, then you can catch yourself when you're in them. Then you can ask yourself if you are doing the thing because it makes your heart happy, or if you're trying to self-soothe. It then becomes your choice as to what you do. Are you following your heart or not? If so, wonderful! If not, will you choose to follow your old patterns that you'll likely kick yourself for later, or will you choose to make a change? If you find yourself in old patterns, show yourself compassion and be gentle with yourself, and recognize you can choose a different option next time. Patterns take time to change, and they'll come around over an over again. But with each return, you'll have a greater level of awareness and see things from a higher perspective.

Do know that this is not a one-time thing… you'll have to go through this process over and over again. Again, it's a practice. Check in with your heart in all you do. It will guide you to your best life. If something calls to you, then listen to the nudge. If something doesn't sit right, your heart is telling you it's not in alignment with you. Sit with that and think about or journal through the feelings attached to this. You'd be surprised what your heart will tell you… if you listen.

Coaching, Mentoring, and Counseling

Early on, I spent years in therapy and it was very helpful at identifying and discussing relevant issues in my life. One thing I found, however, is that I always felt I didn't have enough time. Just as I was getting to the important things, my time would end. But it did allow me to continue processing on my own. The other observation I made was that I would only go as deep as I chose. The therapist didn't push me to look deeper, so eventually I found that I was spinning my wheels as I didn't know how to crack the layers yet untouched.

Therapy certainly had its place, and I benefitted from it. I encourage anyone to find a therapist you trust where you can express your emotions… it's fantastic for that. That is what therapy

I designed for. However, if you are like me and searching for more answers, alternative routes are available.

I've been blessed in recent years to work with three absolutely incredible coaches. They've been able to cut through what I felt was the main issue and help me see where the real issues were. This is where I've made my greatest progress and break throughs. My coaches provided a safe space to really be raw, to push me to places I could never have reached on my own. They asked the hard questions to guide me to see the truths about myself and find acceptance of them. Therapists are limited by the rules of practice and just can't go there. Coaches can, and mine did so with complete respect, ethics, and love.

My first two coaches, Megan and Renee of Kindred, worked with me for four years. I had several coaching packages with them, as well as workshops and their online groups. I discovered my inner child with them in Disneyland during their inner child workshop. I learned what my core values were… acceptance and love, and what my purpose is… to assist others in their own healing. I found my authentic self and felt what it was like to be accepted for exactly who I am, without being asked to change. The Kindred community was my family, where I learned I could be myself without chameleoning as I had done in the past. I healed so much of myself during this time, and it was a true turning point in how I saw myself.

My third coach, Kerry, has expanded on the work I did with Megan and Renee. She's helped me further connect to myself and listen to what my body is telling me. She's helped me to be even further empowered and tap into my own energy to stand in my full power. It all comes back to listening to yourself… being in balance with your heart and mind. Most importantly, listening to what they have to tell you. All answers are truly within you, one merely has to listen to them! Spirit is always guiding us, and messages come particularly to your heart, as that is, and should be our guiding force.

I will never regret working with these amazing coaches, and they have given me the tools to become a coach, myself. They are as inspiring as they are effective in getting their clients to achieve their goals. The key is that they've been there, too. They practice what they preach, as do I. Growth and healing is a continuous process and I now have all the tools I need to keep going strong.

Chapter Twelve: Finding Myself

I was in my forties when I first discovered that I didn't really know who I was. I'd spent my entire life up to this point being what other people expected me to be. Not just specific people, but also society in general. I tried to fit the mould. I was a follower, a people pleaser, a yes girl. I excelled in school, went on to university, got married, and started a family because that was what one was supposed to do, right? I felt pressure to do all the things. I never stopped to ask myself if any of these things were actually what I wanted, what my soul called for.

It wasn't until I began with coaching that I realized I was living my life for other people, and not for myself. That's when the shift began. It didn't happen overnight but built up until I couldn't ignore the call anymore. My soul was calling for freedom… freedom to discover who I was and what I was meant for in this world.

What?! I Have a Choice?

It was mind blowing to realize that I didn't have to live the life I had been living all this time… that I actually had the full choice to live the life I wanted, not the life expected of me. Realizing I had the choice opened new doors in my life. I was able to start exploring what made me, me… what fueled my heart, what I was meant to be in this life. I'd never even considered this before. With choice, came the freedom to begin to discover my infinite potential and to be free to be me, unapologetically.

This didn't come without tough decisions, however. I left the security of a sixteen-year marriage, to, for the first time ever, make it on my own. My first husband is an amazing man, and I can't say enough good things about him, but my heart screamed to be free. It was terrifying to say I needed to leave, especially as we have three amazing boys together. I worried how it would affect them… if I would damage them by leaving. As it turns out, it was the best outcome for all of us. I've now been able to be the best me for my children, and the best friend I could be for my ex-husband.

This decision was both terrifying and freeing all at the same time. I knew I had to take care of myself first, or I'd never live up to my potential. I needed this opportunity to solely work on myself… the soul that had been lost all this time. I needed to choose me. This was the first time I'd made decisions for myself as opposed to deferring to someone else. It took practice, a lot of it, to begin to trust my choices, as I was new to it. It was a process of trial and error in discovering what were choices that worked for me, and ones that weren't the greatest, but even in those choices were learning opportunities.

I made mistakes along the way with money, in prioritizing going out all the time over sitting with myself and going within, as a parent, and with who I welcomed into my life. But I got there, as each blip brought awareness to what I wanted to do differently the next time.

The biggest lesson I learned was to follow my heart, my intuition, as it has always led me in the right direction. It took some time to tap into this knowledge, but now that I have, there's been no going back. Sometimes my head likes to get in the way and logic myself out of what feels right, even if it makes no sense to anyone else. But I've learned it doesn't matter whether it makes sense or not, my heart always leads me to where it needs to be, even if it's not linear... life tends not to be linear anyhow. My heart guides me to the next right thing every time, as long as I get out of my own way.

Along with now making choices for myself, comes the accountability and responsibility for those choices. They are mine alone, I can't place blame on anyone if I make a choice that I don't end up liking. I have to accept my faults and hold myself accountable, but that is all part of the deal... owning my choices no matter what. And now as I make choices that are aligned with what feels right in my heart, it is so empowering. I no longer worry about what others think of my choices, as my opinion is the only one that matters. It's my life, my personal journey to experience, after all.

Finding My Inner Child Again

Now, I'm a girl who never grew up as the typical creative, imaginative child. I didn't know how to. When I got toys, I set them up like they were on the box, and then they sat on the shelf. I didn't have a clue what to do with them after that. As my siblings played make believe, I watched in awe as I had no idea how they managed to be so imaginative.

Not understanding how to connect to others left me feeling isolated, alone, different… broken somehow. I wanted to be included, but just had no idea how to do the normal kid stuff. I felt like an outsider looking in with longing to be the same. But my inner child was lost at that point and I simply didn't know how to have fun.

So, I got lost in books. I could get lost in a plot no problem. The descriptiveness in books was the creativity I lacked. I'd pick up a book and read not put it down again until I completed it. Books were the friends I didn't feel I had. The characters each owning a piece of my heart. In books I found comfort, solace, and support.

We all have an inner child, who, most likely needs some love and healing from us as adults. Our inner child is that pure spirit, the one who finds joy in hopping in puddles and smelling the fresh scent of spring flowers in the air. Our inner child is also the one who is fragile and needing protection, as they are so innocent.

I've spent a lot of time connecting to and healing my inner child these past years. She's been walled up within me for forty years. When we experience traumas as a child, it affects our inner child immensely. She needs to feel safe and secure. My inner child didn't feel safe, so I walled her off to keep her safe, as that's the only way I knew how to protect her at the time. Only a few years ago, did she feel safe enough to come out.

Through reiki, soul retrieval, and heart forging, I became whole, and my inner child began to feel safe. She is my center of joy, the pure innocence of the spirit. I now regularly meet with her in meditation to confer with what she wants. My highest self is also part of this tea party. We sit down and they tell me what they are needing at that time. Then I use their wisdom to do what fuels my soul, makes us all happy, and leads me to my best life.

Even as I worked with my inner child as I stated above, I still found it very difficult to know how to play. I was an old soul even as a child, spending more time observing others as opposed to acting like a child… playing and using my imagination. When I tried, my mind was blank. So, I didn't. I read and did crafts, like coloring pictures already drawn. God help me if I was asked to freehand draw something or write about something without a topic provided. I'd have nothing come to me.

I also felt it was my responsibility as the oldest of five to be the responsible one. Even when my family went to Disneyland when I was twelve, I foreboded joy. I didn't like the rides because I'd get headaches and nauseous. I was "too old" to wear Mickey ears or dare to have fun. I also had a very difficult time tapping into my inner child because I had her so walled off. I didn't see the magic all around me, and it's really sad, when you think about it. I got the opportunity to have a do-over, however.

The most profound and monumental experience in my personal growth came when Kindred held a workshop for connecting with your inner child, and we were to go to Disneyland to do so. At this time, February of 2019, I'd learned about my inner child and was ready to connect with her. I knew this was an important part of my journey. So, I signed up without hesitation.

For the retreat, I set the intention to view everything through the eyes of a child, to look at my surroundings with the wonder and awe I hadn't allowed myself to view anything in life with up to that point. The retreat began with a conference, tapping into our inner child and listening to her needs and wants. Healing the past hurts and making her feel safe to come show me how to play. We were gifted party favors like a little girl's birthday party with sashes, glow sticks, candies, and more.

Then we hit the streets of Disneyland, and my heart was fully open to receiving the joy and magic of being there. I was also blessed with doing so with my friends from Kindred. Nobody was ever left out, and the time flew by. We all got to meet out favorite characters, eat whatever we wanted, and I even bought a crown to wear. I felt like being a princess, and princesses wore crowns! I still put it on at times to tap into the childlike energy I found there.

Sunday, our last day at the park, was pure magic. My energy was in flow, and I was enjoying myself completely. I didn't hold back from anything I wanted to do, and neither did the ladies I was with. Within the span of two hours, it seemed everyone's dreams came true. Everyone met their characters, even ones who rarely made an appearance. The marching band played in front of the castle, and we happened to be front and centre as they played songs of friendship and love, and we cried tears of joy. We took a group picture just after, and you can see the joy on all our faces. There were no fake smiles there.

As I've mentioned before, I never really got in touch with my authentic self until recently. Well Disneyland was the first time she presented herself. By tapping into my inner child, I allowed myself to simply be. This led to the most memorable moment of my life, and it's been a complete game changer.

Now, part of the Disneyland experience was a treasure hunt of sorts. One of the challenges was to buy a balloon, and gift it to whoever your heart called you to present it to. Well, as a group of us came off the Matterhorn ride, Renee and Megan, our mentors, were waiting for us, and in Megan's hand was a purple balloon with a bunch of characters on it. As we approached them, Megan and Renee pulled me aside, and presented me with the message that I was loved and accepted completely as I was. They saw my authentic self even when I hadn't, and they honored my inner child who had finally come out to play. Well, tears flowed everywhere… I was bawling, holding onto Megan for dear life, Renee and Megan had tears, and the other girls couldn't keep it together, either. Even as I type this, the tears flow in memory of that moment, and I am forever grateful.

It is and will forever be known as the "Balloon Moment" where I finally realized I was worthy and accepted just for being me. My inner child was overflowing with joy. I carried that balloon like a badge of honor, finding true childlike joy in the receiving of it and having it with me. I had found myself and it was absolutely incredible. There was no turning back, now.

Balloon Family

As I've grown, I have come to realize that the number of friends isn't what's important, it's the quality of the friends you have. As I was seen and accepted in Disneyland simply for being me, led me to curate a family, not based on blood, but of unconditional acceptance.

Thus the "Balloon Moment" led to the creation of my balloon family. These are the divine individuals who see me and fully accept me for who I am, no strings attached. The humans that don't judge me for mistakes I've made but accept my light and darkness. And I do my very best to do the same for them.

First and foremost, Renee and Megan of Kindred will always be cherished in my heart as they love me unconditionally and were the ones to help me see it for myself. The Kindred community, in particular the Moving Forward crew, add to my balloon family. We've held space for each other, been raw and vulnerable with each other, grown together, and support each other as we go on.

My first husband is still a soul mate of mine, a cherished friend, who also accepts, supports, and wants the best for me. My best friend, and soul sister is most certainly part of this family. She and I have traveled such similar paths and can pretty much read each other's minds. The last person to note, is my other coach, Kerry. She's a being of light and supports me, roots me on, and wants only the best for me at the balloon family level.

As new people enter my life, I am careful to determine if they fit into my circle. I no longer seek to fit into other circles, I've curated my own. One where honesty and safety is key. I value my energy and my circle reflects those that fuel my energy as opposed to draining it. And as I evolve, I've let go and shed those who aren't growing with me. I hold no resentment and let them go with love, but I allow myself to move on, making space for the balloon people to find their way to me.

Listening to My Heart and Getting Out of My Head

One of the best pieces of advice I was given by an amazing woman, Sonia Choquette, was to get out of my head and listen to my heart. My head was a bad neighborhood to live in as our brains like to trick us and logic us out of attaining the divine experiences our hearts are leading us to.

Ever since that discussion, I have remembered that. Now, our head, our ego, is simply doing its job of keeping us safe, but there is little growth in safety. I choose to grow and live the very best life I can, and my heart is the guide for that. Yes, it takes trust and faith, but I have never been steered wrong. Even when something seems odd, I go with it. And by doing so I've had wonderful experiences and one step has led to another and another, these odd pieces actually weaving together creating a beautiful life. I couldn't anticipate or try to foresee these events fitting together, but they do when you listen to your heart.

Our heads like logic and reason whereas our hearts are connected to the divine. When we pause and ask ourselves what our heart wants decision by decision, we are allowing ourselves to be guided by the Source that wants the very best for us. This is when life feels easy because we are in flow. We are in alignment with our soul's desires and allowing ourselves to listen to our hearts and nourish our souls.

I now ask my heart in the moment... What do I need? And then I follow through. Sometimes I need to move my body, sometimes it's to rest, sometimes it's to take a drive, and sometimes it's the need to reach out to someone that's been on my mind. It has become as easy as recognizing when I am hungry or need to go to the bathroom. My life is so much more enriched by where my heart has led me.

Awareness of what the heart wants is the key to this, and it comes with practice. You can start with yes and no questions to get the feel of how your heart communicates with you. You can ask yourself if you want a cup of coffee, whether you are hungry, and if so, what is your heart wanting to eat? Then do the thing. This builds trust with what your heart is saying and can be a fun game, too. Be sure to take note of the adventures and synchronicities that come into your life when you allow yourself to follow your heart.

Believing in Myself

Believing in myself has been a lifelong struggle. I received so many messages that contradicted my own instincts, that it built doubt. The negative messages I received and then told myself about my body and self worth stripped my confidence. And not truly knowing who I was made it difficult to make decisions that were in alignment with my heart.

Several factors changed this for me, however. First of all I found myself… the core values that guide me, my purpose in life, and that I am perfect just as I am, right now, every moment. Radically accepting that I don't have to be anything other than who I am, was mind blowing, and completely freeing at the same time. I no longer carry the weight of trying to be more than I am.

I was able to heal the negative messaging I'd received in the past, letting go of the hold they once had on me. I listened to my heart, and followed through, building trust with myself and discovered that my decisions are sound ones. Do I slip up sometimes? Sure, I'm human, but rather than beating myself up about it, I have learned to show myself grace and compassion, and I move on. I don't view them as mistakes any longer, but as opportunities for learning.

I have given myself the permission to explore what makes me happy, breaking out of the deep conditioning that I once lived under. I have discovered so much about myself and look at the world with curiosity and wonder. I set intentions for myself every morning and show great gratitude for all the blessings that come to me each day. I've established trust with myself through daily practice and trial and error. I'm more focussed on what makes my heart happy than once tying my happiness to a certain weight. I accept and love my good side, and my dark side, both being worthy of my love. I accept myself for who I am, deep down, not just the person I want to be. I no longer hide from myself, and I embrace all that makes me, me… unapologetically.

The Water, The Trees, and Me

One of my favorite things to do to connect with myself and my heart, is to get back to nature. This is where I nourish my soul, where I connect to the Universe without distraction, and where I am at peace.

My heart takes me barefoot, walking the deer trails down by the river. My feet connected to the Earth, grounding me as I talk with the trees and take solace amongst them. I hug them and share my love with them and listen to their whispers. They hold great knowledge if you're listening. I wade at the river's edge, feeling its current flowing, carrying away all worries with it. Feeling the caressing water reminding me that all things are connected. Feeling its powerful yet gentle energy.

My body soaks up the energy of the sun, but my heart bursts at the sight of the moon, my lifelong love. I've always had an unexplainable connection to the moon, and I celebrate her when she is full and when she is new again. She calls to me like she is calling me home. I am connected to everything, and everything is connected to me.

Chapter Thirteen: Who I Am Now

As I hope I've demonstrated throughout the pages of this book that it is never too late to find yourself and live your best life. You merely need to choose to do something about your situation and know there are supports for you out there. My wish is that these pages have been a source of support and inspiration to you all. That you can look back and take your own steps, listening to your heart and creating your own best life, whatever that looks like for you. And know that the Universe is always looking out for you and wanting the best for you, you need only to ask it for help.

The Sum of All Parts

I've gone from a scared, insecure, shame-driven individual, to living a life of empowered decisions. I have put in the hard work of facing my own demons and embracing them as part of what makes me who I am. I follow my heart even when others may not understand it, but it's not for them to understand, I am the only one that I need to be accountable to. I no longer live in fear, but in freedom. I love myself and know who I am. My life is full of possibility and all I have to do is follow my heart to achieve my goals.

I trust myself, believe in myself, and validate myself. I am the source of my own happiness, no longer seeking it from outside sources. I am at peace with myself and enjoy my own company. I spend time listening to what my heart tells me and pay attention to my instincts. I take care of myself as I would take care of my children, resting, nourishing my body, mind, and soul, and being gentle with myself. I show myself kindness and treat myself like my own best friend.

Anything is Possible

When you are in a state of flow, in tune with yourself and the Universe, anything is possible. All your dreams can come true. You merely have to set the intention, do the work you need to do on yourself and towards your goal, and let the Universe do the rest.

I've been there and done it, so I'm not just pulling this out of thin air. I've worked hard on myself to clear any blocks preventing me from achieving my dreams. I step forward fearlessly, trusting that I will always be supported by the Universe and that the right people will enter my life at the right time. So far this has been the case. I've manifested people, money, and experiences that I desired. I even have a specific manifestation book. I call in what I want and let go of the outcome, allowing Spirit to figure out the details. And every time a manifestation comes to fruition, I show tremendous gratitude for it.

Knowing what my heart desires and following the nudges has been the greatest success in being where I am now. I know who I am and what I want, and I will not settle, whether that be in love, finances, or life. I'm willing to wait for what I want and enjoy my life as it is in the meantime.

When you trust yourself and the Universe, it is truly amazing what comes into your life. The biggest thing is to recognize all the blessings as they come, and appreciate what life is trying to offer you. The Universe wants to help you, to give you all you desire, you just need to invite the help in and then follow through on your end. This has been my practice, and I believe the world is my oyster... and this is only the beginning!

The Witch, The Lion, and The Phoenix

I am a very Spiritual person, as you might have recognized. I believe that we are always guided by the Universe, and that my purpose is to use my connection to Spirit to help others. I was guided to write my story to inspire and bring hope to others, and to be available to coach those who feel called to reach out to me.

I call myself witchy... I love crystals, sage, reading oracle cards, and the moon. I am highly intuitive, and just know things I shouldn't. I am a Reiki Master and psychic. I believe in spirits and ethereal beings others cannot see. All these tools help me in my journey and connect me to Spirit. It is a large part of who I am and I embrace it regardless of what others may think. I know myself and who I am, and this is a big part of my life. The connection has helped me overcome so much!

I always had gut feelings about things and was very rarely surprised by things as I just knew what was going on. I was raised Orthodox but found the works of Sylvia Browne really resonate with my belief of the Universe. The notion of hell and punishment didn't sit with me. If our Higher Power loved us as I believe, then why would we ever be sent to eternal damnation? I also believe we choose the life we come into, including the people and experiences we have in order to grow and learn, and that we have all lived many lives in many worlds.

I have really extended my intuition over the last five years. We all have the capacity for this, it is merely a matter of paying attention and practice. I am not only intuitive, but psychic and a medium as well. What this means is that I have intuitive hits for myself, but I have the capability to connect with other people's energies and their loved ones that have passed. This provides me the honor of being able to deliver messages to individuals from their beloveds.

As a Reiki Master, I am blessed to be the conduit for Spirit to send healing energy to myself and to others. I take great pride in being able to do this work. Not only do I play a role in delivering Reiki energy, but my intuition allows me to share with my clients the source of their blockages or health issues. It is truly a gift to be able to serve the Divine in this way.

Phoenix Rising

I have a large Spirit team, headed by my main guide, Ben. He's always with me and rallies the troops when I need their extra support. I also have a mother tree where I connect and find solace when I need to be comforted, her branches and roots wrapping around me in her embrace. Her base is where I hold my meetings with the rest of my Spirit Team.

Leo, my beloved lion, has been a source of strength, courage, and empowerment for me all my life. He has stepped back in his role in the last year or so as I have been able to be empowered for myself, being strong and courageous within myself. But he continues to check in on me, letting me know he's never far away.

I am strong, brave, and true to my heart. This is my compass, what guides me to overcome anything I encounter. I love who I am at the core, not the chameleon. I don't need to do that anymore as I know my own self now. I embrace all parts of me, and use them as strengths. Leo reminds me of this.

Amber, a phoenix, is also part of my Spirit team, and reminds me of the fact that I have all the tools I need within me to continue to rise. When an obstacle pops up, I rise like the phoenix rises from its own ashes to become even stronger. I have a sense of determination and persistence that cannot be denied, and when I want to accomplish something, nothing gets in my way. The phoenix also reminds me that even in the darkest of times, I always have the strength to rise.

Just as the title of this book indicates, I am Phoenix Rising. I will overcome any obstacles in my path and live my best life. I cherish my strength and determination, and the guidance I've had along the way. My journey is not over yet, but whatever comes my way, I know I am supported and more than capable of rising to the occasion.

May you rise too.

Manufactured by Amazon.ca
Bolton, ON